CREATIVE RESOURCES FOR YOUTH MINISTRY

Creative Activities
for Small Youth Groups

CREATIVE RESOURCES FOR YOUTH MINISTRY

Creative Activities for Small Youth Groups

Compiled by Wayne Rice and Mike Yaconelli
Edited by Yvette Nelson

Saint Mary's Press
Christian Brothers Publications
Winona, Minnesota

The contents of this book are reprinted with permission from *Ideas,* vol. 44, *Great Ideas for Small Groups,* and *Creative Socials and Special Events,* published by Youth Specialties (Grand Rapids, MI: Zondervan Publishing House, 1988, 1986, 1986).

The publishing team for this book included Robert P. Stamschror, development editor; Mary Duerson Kraemer, copy editor; Maura C. Goessling, production editor; David Piro, cover designer; pre-press, printing, and binding by the graphics division of Saint Mary's Press.

Printed in the United States of America

Printing: 8 7 6

Year: 2004 03 02

ISBN 0-88489-264-6

 Genuine recycled paper with 10% post-consumer waste.
Printed with soy-based ink.

Contents

Introduction

Part 1: Learning Activities

Part 2: Quiet Games for Small Places

Part 3: Indoor Action Games ━━━━━

Part 4: Outdoor Action Games ━━━━━

Part 5: Relays and Races

Part 6:
Special Events and Social Activities

Part 7:
Service Projects for Small Youth Groups

Introduction

Youth Ministry Today: Its Growth and Development

For the past twenty years, Catholic youth ministry has been in the process of critically re-examining its philosophy, goals, and principles. In part, this re-examination grew out of the perceived and felt needs of young people who will be the adults of the twenty-first century. In the early seventies—before youth ministry, as we know it, existed— those who worked with young people saw a need to experiment with new styles and forms of ministry with young people. Many parishes, schools, and dioceses began to develop youth ministries on the solid foundation of relational ministry and on the unique social and developmental needs of young people. Heretofore they had relied on the unquestioned process of presenting organizational, programmatic approaches such as weekly or biweekly classes, sports programs, or rarely, weekend or overnight retreats.

The new processes and approaches planted and tended during those years produced a renewed ministry with young people based on experience and insight. Leaders in the field of youth ministry discovered that ministry with young people must be a multifaceted, comprehensive, and coordinated effort. They rediscovered the age-old truth of Jesus' ministry: all ministry is rooted in relationships. Through the leaders' outreach and relationship building, young people began to experience the warmth of an accepting community, which is vital for the development of a comprehensive youth ministry. As relationships grew, a sense of belonging and participation also grew. The experience of acceptance, belonging, and participation opened young people so that they were able to reveal the needs and the concerns that preoccupied them. Programs developed around these needs and concerns: service projects, retreats, new forms of catechesis, peer ministry, prayer groups, celebrations of the sacraments. With these rediscovered opportunities for ministry, youth ministers were in a position to help young people grow personally and spiritually and find their place in the faith community as active Catholic Christians with a mission.

As the style of youth ministry changed, the traditional ministry to young people by the community evolved into a fourfold approach. Youth ministry was conceived not only in terms of responding *to* the unique social and developmental needs of young people but also in terms of adults' sharing a common ministry *with* young people, *by*

■ 9

young people (especially involving their peers), and *for* young people (adults interpreting young people's legitimate concerns and acting as advocates for them). This fourfold understanding—to, with, by, and for—changed the style and broadened the scope of youth ministry.

In 1975 and 1976, hundreds of youth leaders from across the country consulted for fifteen months and concretized the aims and philosophy of youth ministry in a document called *A Vision of Youth Ministry*. It has served to guide the church's mission to young people ever since. *A Vision of Youth Ministry* affirmed the growth that had taken place and challenged the whole church to renew itself.

The document clearly places youth ministry within the framework of the mission and ministry of the church. It defines youth ministry as the "response of the Christian community to the needs of young people, and the sharing of the unique gifts of youth with the larger community."[1] This reciprocal relationship helps the community to view youth ministry as part of the entire ministry of the community, not separate from it—a problem often encountered when a ministry with young people is perceived as a club or an organization set apart from the mainstream of church life. *A Vision of Youth Ministry* makes clear that an effective ministry with young people incorporates them into the life of the community, where they can share their gifts and talents with the whole community. If young people are to have positive experiences of church life, they must have opportunities to be involved in the whole life of the community. Such opportunities for this type of interaction are at the heart of youth ministry, not on the periphery. By being involved in the church life with adults, young people gain a view of what it means to be an adult Catholic Christian. This is a special gift of adults to young people.

The categories of youth ministry as outlined in *A Vision of Youth Ministry* closely parallel the fundamental ministries of the church: word, worship and celebrating, creating community, and service and healing.[2] The seven categories of youth ministry describe the forms that this ministry should take. It is a common framework for a holistic ministry with young people. Briefly, the seven components of youth ministry are as follows:[3]

Word: proclaiming the Good News that leads young people to faith in Jesus (evangelization) and deepening a young person's faith in Jesus and applying that faith to their everyday life (catechesis)

Worship: celebrating relationships in community and with the Lord through a variety of worship experiences, personal prayer, and spiritual development

Creating community: building relationships with young people and creating a healthy environment for growth, in which young people can experience acceptance, belonging, and participation

Guidance and healing: responding to young people's need for spiritual, moral, and personal counseling; vocational guidance; and reconciliation with self, others (peers and family), and God

Justice and service: educating young people to the demands of justice and the social problems of our world, responding to young people who suffer injustice, and motivating young people for service on behalf of others

Enablement: calling forth adults and young people to become ministers and providing them with the understanding and skills needed for effective ministry

Advocacy: working on behalf of young people, interpreting their concerns and needs, and standing up for them in the Christian, and larger, community

Youth ministry has experienced a renewal within the U.S. Catholic church. A renewed ministry with young people brings a need for new and better resources to assist leaders. Before turning to the resources found in this book, let's examine the place of creative social and learning strategies within youth ministry.

Creative Strategies for Youth Ministry

We have already seen the primacy of relationships in youth ministry. However, as relationships grow and programs are created, strategies are needed to accomplish youth ministry's tasks. The strategies in this book are aids. Their aim is to provide you with a variety of activities you can use in any number of programs. Some of these strategies are primarily suited for one or another component of youth ministry. However, most are adaptable to any number of components. All these strategies foster a particular type of learning—experiential learning. To understand its contribution to your youth ministry, let's examine experiential learning.

Experiential Learning

We have often heard it said that we learn from experience. This is true to an extent. But so much of our own life experience goes by without us ever learning from it. If young peoples' life experiences are to be sources of learning and growth, then young people must reflect upon and assimilate them. This often goes undone because no one takes time to help them reflect upon those experiences and learn from them. In addition to life experience, there is a second source of experiential learning: structured experiences. Experiences we develop that engage young people in the learning process and enable them to reflect are a rich resource for learning.

The structured experiences found in the Creative Resources series—communication games, learning strategies, simulations, projects, case studies, planning ideas, crowd-breakers, mixers, games, special events, and skits—are potential learning experiences for young people.

Creative Gaming

Creative games can serve many purposes in youth ministry. They can acquaint people with one another, build trust, encourage spontaneity, mix and blend groups, and help people release energy. At the same time, they can be fun and learning experiences. Through creative games we discover an opportunity to play *with* instead of *against* one another, thus allowing us to play as a unit and reach a common goal. This type of play lets us learn from and laugh at our mistakes, instead of hiding them away in embarrassment. Creative games enhance the growth of a group and create a feeling of accomplishment among the participants, while providing an enjoyable experience for them.

Cooperative Versus Competitive Games

For many years, competition-winning has been the name of the game in our society. All our organized sports are competitive, sometimes violently so. We encourage good sportsmanship and working together as a team, but the goal is always "Beat the other team, as badly and as hard as possible." It sometimes appears that the biggest and the best players actively compete while the meek and the mild people take their places in the stands, cheering for the physical prowess of those who are "better" than they. Competition can foster an "I am a winner" or "I am a loser" self-concept in people.

Many young people suffer from a poor self-concept. "I am too short to play basketball," "I am too heavy to run track," or "They only like me because I can make fifteen points a game" are statements we often hear from young people. "Winners" and "losers" alike may be scarred by such stereotyped images of themselves. How many adults do we know who still hold on to their childhood dream of being a

pitcher in a World Series game or a quarterback in the Super Bowl? Those dreams will most likely never come true for them because they "just aren't good enough." At least that is what they believe after numerous "failures" on the field at the hands of those who are a little faster, can jump a little higher, or are more agile. Just as many adults do, many young people dream of someday "making it" and harbor an image of themselves as inadequate.

There are appropriate times and places for competitive games of basketball or volleyball, but these games may not be suitable for a break at a retreat. They may be inconsistent with the message and the values we are trying to communicate to young people.

Competitive sports can, and often do, alienate some people who might otherwise participate in group activities. Competitive games are difficult for some people and are often segregating. We see boys playing on one field and girls playing on the other. Sexism in rec-reation can be a divisive factor in the broad set of values we try to communicate.

For the most part, the games in this book are cooperative in character.

Principles for Cooperative Gaming

1. Games are an effective educational tool. The primary purpose of games and play is to have fun. However, we do learn during play. We learn what is and what is not acceptable behavior, for example. When young people take part in a sport, they also watch the spectators. Their observations may tell them that certain language or actions are appropriate or that others are inappropriate and may even warrant penalties. In cooperative sports, young people learn how to work as a unit, how to cooperate with one another to achieve a desired goal.

Creative sports teach us new and exciting things about ourselves and others. We learn the advantages of working together instead of trying always to win. We learn the place of healthy competition by working together. Putting competition in its proper perspective becomes an insightful experience. Cooperative games teach us skills and encourage leadership, and they enable us to grow while learning.

2. Games are an extension of the values we communicate. In cooperative gaming, we remove the element of competition and replace it with the value of working together. If caring and sharing are values we are trying to communicate to young people, then a cooperative game allows those values to be lived out even in play. There is no competing, no trying out for teams, no choosing of captains; no one is left out. No one is more important than anyone else because everyone is a vital part of the unit.

If we are trying to build community with young people but encourage competitive sports during recreation time, we contradict ourselves immediately. Cooperative games are an extension of our values: we respect each person, we work together, we have fun, and no one gets hurt.

3. Cooperative games build community and help us minister to one another. Cooperative games build a sense of community among participants. By working together and tapping one another's gifts and strengths, people discover new relationships.

Ministry happens during playtime: We encourage one another, work together, laugh, struggle, and ultimately succeed *together*. Often, the people who are ministered to during cooperative sports are those who have been left to sit in the stands before because "they weren't good enough to play." The "stars" are also ministered to because they don't feel the pressure of having to produce "points." They can play, cooperate, enjoy, be encouraged, and struggle along with the group.

4. Cooperative games encourage leadership. In cooperative play, no one is *appointed* leader because he or she is stronger, bigger, or brighter. Leadership is granted by the group, at the pace of the group, and when the need is recognized by the members. Leadership emerges by consensus, and it often develops nonverbally. Cooperative recreation encourages leadership and allows it to grow and be fostered by the group members. There is perhaps nothing more exciting to watch than the dynamics of interaction in cooperative games as young people try to conquer the obstacle at hand—and experience delight in their accomplishment. Cooperative play opens up the exciting possibilities of working as a unit, getting along, and complementing one another, as well as having fun.

5. Cooperative gaming allows the development of skills. Many people playing cooperative games have a difficult time until someone says, "I don't feel we are listening to one another. If we talk one at a time and listen, we will be able to figure this out more quickly." As the group discovers more effective means of communicating, it develops a sense of problem solving and decision-making, skills that are important to growth.

6. Cooperative games allow everyone to feel a sense of importance and accomplishment. Cooperative games allow everyone to play and work together. People are not left out because they are too short, too fat, too slow, or the "wrong" sex. Everyone is given the opportunity to feel accepted and needed instead of fearing rejection or the pressure of having to prove something to the group. *Everyone* is included in the activity. Everyone is an important part of the group and is needed by all because of the variety of experiences, personal strengths, gifts, and talents each person brings.

Guidelines for Creative Gaming

1. Always encourage and affirm the participants during games.
2. Model the Christian behavior you are expecting or hoping for from the participants.
3. Avoid games that are sexist, that is, games that assume and promote sexual stereotypes or that use sexist language.
4. Play games that challenge participants to grow, but do not choose games that frustrate the players by their difficulty.
5. Be prepared—have all equipment on hand.
6. Play only games that you personally have "field-tested."
7. Play games that help create a relaxing, comfortable atmosphere; that build community; and that avoid liable risk of bodily harm.
8. Avoid games that misuse things (such as food), waste or harm natural resources, or damage clothing, carpeting, and so on.
9. Clearly explain the object and the rules of a game before beginning (except, of course, in games that require an element of surprise).

Notes

1. United States Catholic Conference (USCC), *A Vision of Youth Ministry* (Washington, DC: USCC, Department of Education, 1976), p. 4.
2. For a contemporary description of the fundamental ministries of the church, see James Dunning, "About Ministry: Sharing Our Gifts," *PACE* 8 (1977) and *PACE* 9 (1978).
3. USCC, *A Vision of Youth Ministry,* p. 7.

PART 1

Learning Activities

Introduction

Although all of life's experiences can be learning experiences, some experiences or activities set out to teach. The activities in this section do just that, but not in a monotonous, wordy sort of way. These activities set out to teach in an involving, enjoyable, creative way. Some of the activities serve to introduce an idea or to get your group's creative juices going. They lure the participants into thinking of new options, putting items or letters together in new and creative ways, encouraging new combinations of participants, opening up new discoveries about one another.

These learning activities can be used as icebreakers, reviews, and eye-openers or for closing a meeting. The activities can be bent, stretched, warmed, cooled, recycled, renewed, recast, and replayed. These learning activities are all yours; take them and run.

Where Do I Stand?

This learning strategy works with almost any topic. You will need six large pieces of colored poster board. The colors of the poster board and their positions on the floor should look like this:

Black	Red	Orange	Yellow	Green	Blue

Agree   Disagree

Think of a number of hypothetical situations that involve making value choices. For example:

■ A baby is born with a serious birth defect that would make him or her unable to live without constant care in an institution. Should the child be allowed to die?

■ A woman is a prisoner in a concentration camp. Her husband and children are waiting for her in a nearby neutral country. The only possible way she can be freed from this prison is to become pregnant because pregnant women are automatically released. Should she have sex with another man so that she can become pregnant?

Read aloud a situation. Tell the young people to decide what they think and to stand on one of the colored squares indicating their decision. Explain that the blue square at one end represents total disagreement and the black square at the other represents total agreement. The other colors represent a continuum between these two extremes. Point out that none of the squares stand for a neutral position. After everyone has chosen a place to stand, ask each person to share why she or he feels this way. During the discussion, tell the young people that they may move to a different square. If everyone agrees, the entire group will be standing on one of the squares. This is all right, but it is not your goal. The goal is first of all to allow the young people the opportunity to think through some of their values and to see them in relation to the values of others.

Read aloud another situation and proceed as before.

The A-Team

A-Team stands for "Answer Team." This problem-solving exercise stimulates discussion. Before you begin, write a number of problems or questions (like those that follow) on slips of paper and place them in a bowl. Then have the participants divide into A-Teams, which should be no larger than three or four.

Have each team draw a question from the bowl and go somewhere to work on a solution or an answer. Allow approximately ten minutes for this. When the teams return, have each team read its problem or question and share its response. The rest of the group can decide whether they agree with the answer. If there is disagreement, have the group discuss the issue.

1. I don't get it. If Christianity is true, why are there so many religions that call themselves Christian? I mean, what is the difference between Baptists, Catholics, and so on?

2. If you ask me, the Christian religion makes you a doormat, always loving and turning the other cheek.

3. What if I lived like hell for eighty years and then became a Christian on my deathbed? Would Pope John Paul II and I go to the same place?

4. Your father says this to you: "Your mother and I do not believe in all this Jesus stuff, and we think you spend too much time in church. So we want you to stay away from church for a while."

5. If God is a god, then why can't we see him or her or it? Why don't you prove that God exists? Go ahead . . . prove it to me.

6. The Bible has some nice little stories in it, but everyone knows it is full of contradictions, errors, and myths. How can you believe it?

7. I know a bunch of people that go to your church, and they are supposed to be Christians. But I also know what they do during the week and at parties that I attend. They are phonies. If Christianity is so great, why are there so many phonies?

8. My little brother died of leukemia, and I prayed like crazy. Don't tell me there is a God who loves us. Why didn't God help my brother?

9. Look, I know I am overweight, and even though it hurts me to say it, I'm ugly. I started coming to your church because I thought the kids in your youth group would treat me differently than the kids do at school. Wrong! They ignore me and make fun of me just like everyone else.

10. My parents make me go to church. I like the youth program, but the Mass is a drag. Our priest's homilies are irrelevant and boring, and Mass doesn't relate to me at all.

11. I have always been told that kids who smoke grass and drink really don't enjoy it. I haven't done any of those things partly because I believed that and partly because I didn't think it was a Christian thing to do. At least, I thought that until a few weeks ago. I tried pot and drinking, and it was great. I never had so much fun in my life. How can something so good be bad? Did the people who told me these things were bad lie?

Dear Abby

This activity is a simple yet effective way to give young people the opportunity to minister to one another. It can also provide you with insight into the concerns and problems of individuals in your group.

Give each person paper and a pencil. Instruct the young people to write a "Dear Abby" letter. Direct them to think of an unresolved problem and explain it in letter form to a newspaper columnist like

Abby. Ask them to sign the letter "Confused," "Frustrated," or any other pseudonym.

After everyone has finished, collect the papers and redistribute them so that everyone has someone else's letter. Have each person become Abby and write a helpful answer on the same sheet of paper. Allow plenty of time for this. When the answers are completed, collect the papers once again and read them to the group. Discuss each letter and response and ask the group whether the advice given was helpful. Also ask the group for other solutions to the problems. Young people are often able to give sincere, sensible, and practical help to one another.

Ad Values

Give each person in the group a selection of magazines with plenty of advertisements in them and a list of values like the one below. Have the young people look through the magazines and match the ads with the values on their list. When they see an ad that appeals to a certain value, have them make a mark beside that value. Here is a sample list:
- wealth, luxury, greed
- security (having no worries)
- sexual or physical attractiveness
- intelligence
- conformity (joining the crowd)
- freedom (doing what you want—no responsibility)
- justice, human rights (showing concern for others)
- power, strength
- responsibility
- ego, pride
- status (being looked up to)
- escape
- humility, self-sacrifice
- self-control
- ease, comfort

After everyone has finished, discuss the results. This exercise can sensitize young people to ads. What conclusions can they make about the values that most advertisements present or appeal to? Do these values bring out the best or the worst in people? Do many ads appeal to Christian values?

The Gossip Game

The Scriptures have a great deal to say about the consequences of idle gossip. The following game demonstrates the consequences of spreading rumors.

Three young people leave the room while a fourth person copies (as best as she or he can) onto poster board a picture that she or he is shown. One of the three persons outside comes in and draws the same drawing, using the first person's drawing as the guide, rather than the original. The next person comes in and draws her or his drawing from the second person's, and so on.

The last person's drawing is then compared with the original, which, of course, will hardly resemble the original. Everyone along the line changes the drawing a little, usually omitting or adding what she or he considers important. This game is entertaining as well as revealing and can be followed with a discussion about gossip and communication.

Madison Avenue

To combine fun with learning, get a video camera with sound that can photograph indoors. Divide your group into teams and have them develop a sixty-second commercial to sell Christianity to the world. Make certain that everyone is involved. You might want to encourage them to do a takeoff on a well-known TV commercial, adapting it to Christianity. Within a week or two, view the commercials. The young people will love seeing themselves on film. Then discuss the feasibility of presenting an accurate picture of Christianity in sixty seconds.

A Penny for Your Thoughts

This effective activity gets young people into discussions. Ask each of them to bring twenty pennies and a nickel to the next discussion (topical or general sharing of ideas). Have them sit in a circle around a basket or a bowl. Pose a question and ask each person in the circle to toss in a penny for his or her thoughts on the subject and to share one sentence on it with the group. Explain that if someone wants to interject more than just a sentence, he or she is really putting in his or her two-cents-worth and must put in two cents. Also tell them that if a person cannot think of anything to say, he or she may "four-feit" by throwing in a nickel and taking a penny. Only one four-feit per person is allowed.

When the discussion is over, the money collected can go to a worthy cause.

Paraphrasing the Love Chapter

This activity gives young people the opportunity to put some of their own thoughts into the Christian Testament's chapter on love—1 Corinthians, chapter 13. By doing an exercise such as this with this or any portion of the Scriptures, young people are forced to think through the meaning and application of the passage. Distribute copies of a passage such as the following. Omit key words or phrases but keep the basic idea. Ask the young people to fill in the blanks with whatever they think fits best. Afterward, compare their versions with the original message. Let each person read her or his version to the entire group.

Fill in the blanks as you see fit in this passage from 1 Corinthians, chapter 13.

If I have all the ability to talk about _____, but have no love, then I am nothing but a big mouth. If I have all the power to _____, but have no love, then my life is a waste of time. If I understand everything about _____, but have no love, then I might as well sit in a gutter. If I give away everything that I have, but have no love, then _____. Love is patient, love is kind, love is _____. Love never _____.

The Poor Person's Holy Land Tour

Because this activity requires movement from location to location, it is great for a small youth group. Announce that you are going to take the group on a tour of the Holy Land and then escort them to places that resemble biblical locations (select places that are within walking or driving distance). For example, take them to the tallest building in town and lead a Bible study there about Satan tempting Jesus to jump from the high mountain. The options are endless: a mountainside for the Sermon on the Mount, a garden for the Garden of Gethsemane, an upstairs room for the Last Supper, an old boiler room for the story of the Hebrew children in the fiery furnace, a country road for the story of Paul's experience on the road to Damascus. Using nature as a visual aid is worth a thousand words.

This tour does not have to be done in one day. Remember that you are not limited to meet in one particular place. Anytime you are preparing a lesson from the Scriptures, consider taking the group to a location that can enhance the study.

For example, if you are studying one of Paul's letters from prison, arrange to have your group locked in a jail cell for the study or arrange a guided tour of a jail, a prison, or a juvenile detention facility. It is a sobering experience for most young people, and the scriptural passages suddenly spring to life.

A Progressive Prayer Service

Here is an interesting way to involve young people in prayer. It can be done in a church, in a home, or on a retreat. The possibilities of this activity are unlimited. It works just like a progressive dinner.

A prayer service has a variety of elements. By participating in each element separately and in a different location, you provide a good opportunity to teach young people what worship is. Acts 2:42 and Col. 3:16 provide a good scriptural base. Here is one way to do it.

1. Community: Begin with some kind of group interaction or sharing that provides a chance for the young people to get to know one another better. Create a celebrative but not rowdy mood.

2. Spiritual songs: At the next location, have someone lead the group in a variety of well-known hymns.

3. Prayer: Move to a location that provides a good atmosphere for prayer. If weather permits, a garden would be nice, as Jesus chose a garden for prayer. Have the young people offer prayer requests and thanksgivings.

4. Scriptural reading: At the next location, have several young people read a lesson from the Hebrew Scriptures and the Christian Testament. Use a good translation, such as the New American Bible or the New Jerusalem Bible.

5. Teaching: The next stop can be for the homily. If you prefer, substitute a dialog homily or a film.

Other ingredients, such as the offering, can be incorporated into these stops or additional stops could be added. Design your own progressive paraliturgy, and your group will never forget it.

Sharing Cubes

Make a pair of large dice out of foam rubber or cardboard. On each side of each cube, write an instruction for sharing. Here are some samples:
■ Describe your week.
■ Share a frustration.
■ Share a prayer request.
■ Compliment someone.

Have each person roll a die on the floor. Then have him or her share his or her idea briefly, according to the instruction that turns up. If you have more than eight to ten people in your group, break into smaller groups and give each group one of the dice.

Thanksgiving Exchange

This is a good discussion starter for Thanksgiving or for any time when you want to teach a lesson about gratitude. This exercise helps young people realize that they often take for granted many things for which they should be thankful. It works best with a group whose members know one another fairly well. Begin by having each person share one or two things for which she or he is thankful.

Then have each person write her or his name on the top of a sheet of paper. Collect the sheets and redistribute them so that everyone has a sheet with someone else's name on it. Now have each person write on that sheet what she or he would be thankful for if she or he were the person whose name is on that sheet. The player can list as many things as she or he wants.

Following this, pass the sheets back to the person whose name is on the sheet and discuss the following questions:
- What things are written on your sheet that you have not thanked God for lately?
- What things are written on your sheet that you had not ever thought about thanking God for?
- Is anything written on your sheet that you disagree with or that you do not think you should be thankful for?

Theological Fictionary

If the young people in your group sometimes get stumped trying to figure out the meanings of big theological words, here is a game that will whittle those words down to size.

Make a list of words often used or heard in or around church, such as *liturgy, Eucharist, reconciliation,* and *spirituality.* Write the definition of each on an index card. Take one word at a time and have each person come up with a definition for that word and write it on an index card. If a person is not sure, ask him or her to make up a definition that sounds good. Collect the cards and mix in the correct definition that you wrote out. Read aloud the cards. The object is to guess the correct definition. Announce the scoring as follows:
- five points for a correct definition
- five points for getting agreement on a "phony" definition

As the game progresses, rotate so that each person has a chance to be the first guesser, thus improving the chance that someone will go along with a given definition. The person with the most points is the winner of the game. You will be surprised at the ingenuity of the players in coming up with wild, new theological definitions.

Shopping Spree

For a creative look at money and how people spend it, try this simple simulation with your group. Buy or make several million dollars in play money. Then divide it into random amounts (from $3,000 to $450,000). Place each stack of money in a plain envelope. Pass out the envelopes to your group.

Set up a table or a bulletin board with a wide assortment of full-page advertisements for cars, mansions, computers, gifts, vacations, food, savings accounts, and Christian relief efforts. Put a price tag on each. Give the young people order blanks to buy any items they wish, as long as they can pay for it themselves or can pool their play money to buy it. Give the young people ten minutes to shop and five minutes to fill in their order blanks.

Gather and review all the order blanks. You might list on a chalkboard everything that was ordered. Discuss the values expressed, the participants' feelings about the unequal distribution of the cash and their responsibility to care for others.

American Bandstand

For an effective program about rock music, conduct an American Bandstand activity. Bring in a selection of popular rock records and have the young people vote for the ones they like best, according to certain criteria. This activity can help young people be more sensitive to what they hear. You might find it worthwhile to copy the lyrics so that your group will be able to follow along while listening. Before the young people rate the songs, discuss each of the following three criteria so that they know what each one means:

1. *Lyrics:* What is the message of the song? Does it support or contradict Christian values and the Word of God?
2. *The artist:* What is he or she like as a person? Is the artist a good role model for you? Does he or she avoid behavior that contradicts Christian values?
3. *Overall effect of the song:* Does this song make you feel more positive or more negative about your faith or about life? Does it strengthen you as a Christian, weaken you, or have no effect on you either way?

After the participants have rated all the songs, take your results and come up with your own youth group's Top 10 or Top 5.

Unity

This exercise can help your group understand the concept of unity. Begin by reading Eph. 4:1–16. Discuss with the group members what they think unity means for us today.

Then pass out enough Tinker Toys so that every member of the group has plenty to work with. Ask each person to take his or her Tinker Toys to a place where he or she can work alone to construct something that represents him or her. After they have done this, have everyone return and describe their creation to the rest of the group, explaining the symbolism of their construction, if it is not evident.

Next have the young people pair off. Instruct each pair to try to connect its two Tinker Toy creations into one. After each pair has joined objects, have the pairs get together with other pairs, and continue to join all the objects together until finally they have one big creation. Further discussion may develop. You might want to keep the big Tinker Toy creation on display for a period of time as a reminder to the group of their unity in Christ.

What Others Think of Me

This community-building exercise allows young people to affirm one another and to provide one another with constructive advice. This activity should be used with young people who know one another quite well.

Give each person a slip of paper, approximately three-by-eight inches. Have the young people write their name at the bottom and a one-word self-description at the top. Then have them fold the paper down from the top twice. The paper should look like this:

**Top folded down twice
to conceal the word
written there**

Kim Jones

**Name written
at bottom**

Have the young people exchange their papers twice so that no one knows for sure who has whose paper. Direct each person to leave the paper folded and write immediately below the edge of the fold a one-word description of the person named at the bottom. Urge the young people to be honest, constructive, and helpful. (Tell them that if they do not know the person, they can leave the paper blank.) After they have written on the paper, have them fold it to conceal the word they wrote and exchange the papers again. Repeat the process until the papers are full of one-word descriptions of the person named at the bottom.

Finally, tell the group that when the papers are completed, they are to be returned to the person whose name is at the bottom. Give the young people a few minutes to look their papers over and to compare their self-image with how others think of them. Discussion can follow, with young people sharing their feelings about the exercise and what their response to it will be.

PART 2

Quiet Games for Small Places

Introduction

All the games in this section are designed for use with small groups in confined areas, such as living rooms. The games require relatively little physical activity and are ideal for parties or for warm-ups before youth meetings. These games do require people who are willing to risk a little embarrassment but who are mostly open to a good time. A little bravery and good humor helps, plus a few pencils, some paper, maps, cards, tokens, and other items easily found around a church, a living room, or a den.

Why and Because

Give everyone in the group a pencil and two three-by-five-inch cards. On one card, have them write a question beginning with the word *why*. On the other, have them write an answer that begins with *because*. Collect and redistribute the cards at random and have the players read the question they receive along with the answer. The results can be hilarious.

Bang, You're Dead

This is a game where the leader knows the "secret," and the rest of the group tries to guess it. Everyone is seated around the room in a casual manner, with the leader at the front. After everyone is quiet, the leader raises her or his hand and points it like a gun and says, "Bang, you're dead." The leader then asks the group to guess who was shot. It is hardly ever the person being pointed at. Several people will guess, but they will most likely be wrong. Then the leader announces who it was that was actually shot.

The leader does this several times, changing the pattern of movements each time but consistently pointing a finger at someone and saying, "Bang, you're dead." The players will begin to understand that it is possible to know right away who has been shot and that they have to figure out the secret or clue that leads to the discovery of who actually was shot.

And just what is the secret? The person who was actually shot is the first person to speak after the leader says, "Bang, you're dead." Sooner or later, someone will catch on as the leader perhaps makes it a little more obvious, which might baffle the rest of the group even more. It is fun as well as frustrating.

Bible Family Feud

Well ahead of time, survey an adult study group or social-action group in the parish using questions such as those listed on page 27. Tally the responses to each question. For example, for the question, "Name a disciple of Jesus," the tally might read: Peter, 10; John, 8; Judas, 3; James, 1; Thomas, 1. You will need all the responses tallied and on hand in order to play the game with your youth group. The game is a variation on the TV show "Family Feud."

Create two teams. Have each team send a player to the front. Ask these two players the first question. The team of the player who gives the response that is also the most frequently given response of the adult group (to continue with the example above, the player who responds "Peter") has the option of playing or passing. If it passes, the other team must respond to the next question. The team that opts to play or is given the right to play is allowed only two mistakes while trying to name all the responses (or a maximum of the top six responses given in the adult survey). If the playing team fails to do this,

the opposing team has a chance to steal the round if it can name a correct response not named by the other team. The team winning the most rounds is the winner. Possible questions:
- Name a disciple of Jesus.
- Name one of the Ten Commandments.
- Name a parable of Jesus.
- Name a city in Israel.
- Name one of Saint Paul's letters.
- Name one of the plagues of Egypt.
- Name a famous character from the Hebrew Scriptures.

Chocolate Bar Scramble

Here is a great game for groups of six to ten. A chocolate bar is placed in the center of a table. The candy should be in its wrapper, and to make the game last longer, it can be gift-wrapped as well. Each person sitting around the table takes a turn at rolling the die. The first person who rolls a six gets to start eating the candy bar—but *only* with a knife and a fork. And *only* after he or she has put on a pair of mittens, a cap, and a scarf. And *only* after he or she has run once around the table.

While the person who rolled the six is getting ready to eat the candy bar, the group keeps taking turns rolling the die. If someone else rolls a six, the first person relinquishes his or her right to the candy bar, and the second person must try to eat the candy before someone else rolls a six. The game is over when the entire candy bar is eaten or when everyone drops to the floor with exhaustion!

Confusion Lane

The players sit in a semicircle. The person on one end takes a pencil and hands it to the person sitting next to her or him and says, "Here is a pencil." That person says, "A what?" Then the first person must tell her or him over again. The second person hands the pencil to the third and says, "Here is a pencil." The third person says, "A what?" Then the second person tells the third, "A pencil." This continues all the way around the semicircle. The hard part, however, is that a *different* item is passed in the same way from the other end of the line. When the items meet in the middle, chaos breaks loose.

Touch Telephone

This game is based on the telephone game but involves touch rather than hearing. No talking is allowed. Each group should consist of about six people. Each team sits in a line, one behind the other. The last person is shown a simple hand-drawn picture of an object, such as a house, a cat, or a Christmas tree. Then with his or her fingers he or she tries to draw an exact copy on the back of the person in front of him or her. The drawing can only be done once. The second person draws what he or she felt onto the back of the person in front of him or her. Finally, on a piece of paper the person at the front of the line draws what he or she felt. The team whose picture most resembles the original wins the round.

Geiger Counter

For this game, everyone is seated casually around the room. The leader selects a "volunteer" to leave the room. While she or he is away, the group agrees on a hiding place for a random object that the leader hides. The person then returns and tries to find the object. The rest of the group says "tick-tick-tick-tick" *slower* as she or he moves away from the object and *faster* as she or he moves closer until the object is found. Repeat this with a new contestant each time. The contestant who can find the object in the fastest time wins.

Ring on a String

Direct the group to sit in a circle on chairs and pick one person to stand in the middle. Slip a ring onto a long string and tie the ends together so that you have one large circle with a ring on it that can slide all the way around. Have every person—except the person in the middle—hold a piece of the string with both hands. Tell the group members to slide their hands along the string and pass the ring along as they try to hide it from the person in the middle, who tries to guess who has the ring by walking around the circle and tapping different people's hands. When a person's hand is tapped, he or she opens his or her hands to reveal whether he or she has the ring. When the person in the middle taps someone with the ring, they switch places.

Guess the Ingredients

Copy the ingredients list from a few common items in your pantry or refrigerator. Pass out copies of this list to the young people and have them guess what each item is. Here are a couple of examples:
- soybean oil, eggs, vinegar, water, salt, sugar, and lemon juice (mayonnaise)
- tomatoes, vinegar, corn sweetener, salt, onion powder, and spice (ketchup)

Help Your Neighbor

Young people like to play this card game. You need a minimum of four people. Get several games going if a lot of people want to play. You will need one deck of numbered playing cards for each four people who play. (If you don't have cards numbered through twelve, use regular playing cards and let the jack be number eleven and the queen, number twelve.)

Give everyone a set of cards numbered two through twelve and ask the players to turn the cards face up in front of them.

One person in the group rolls a pair of dice. The player turns over the card that corresponds to the number that was rolled. For example, if the dice total comes to seven, the player turns over his or her number seven card.

The player keeps rolling as long as he or she has cards to turn over. To keep his or her turn alive, the player may turn over the cards of the player on his or her left. The players continue until they can no longer turn over any cards from either their hand or their neighbor's. The game ends when one person has turned over all his or her cards.

Guess Who

For an easy get-acquainted activity, ask each young person to write down something about himself or herself that probably no one else knows. If the young people have trouble coming up with a unique contribution, suggest an unusual pet they might have, or a weird snack or sandwich that they like. If you get really desperate, ask for their mother's middle name. Collect all the responses.

Next, instruct the group to listen to the clues as you read them and try to guess the person they think the clue identifies. Give one thousand points for each correct guess, asking everyone to keep their own score. For a prize, give away a copy of the church directory or a notebook or a journal in which to write down the things they learned about people in the group.

Name Six

For this game, everyone sits in a circle except one person, who sits in the center and closes his or her eyes. An object is passed around until the person in the center claps his or her hands. The person holding the object at that time is assigned a letter by the person in the center. The object is then passed around while the person who was assigned the letter tries to name six things that begin with that letter before the object once again reaches him or her. If unsuccessful, that person must change places with the person in the center of the circle.

Magazine Scavenger Hunt

Divide your group into teams of two or three persons each and give each group a combination of old magazines. Then give them a list of various items, such as photos, names, products, and so on, that can be found in the magazines. As soon as a group finds one of the items, they cut it out and continue to collect as many as they can in the time limit. The list can be long or short depending on the time. Some of the items will be found in several magazines, while others in only one. You can make the list as difficult as you want. The winner, of course, is the team with the most items found.

I Never

This game is not only fun but also fosters communication and openness among young people. Give each person ten tokens of some kind, such as marbles, matches, or pennies. Direct the young people to collect other people's tokens by telling everyone "how life has passed me by." Tell the players to take turns relating a life experience that almost everyone else has had, but they have not, such as riding a roller coaster. Then everyone who *has* done this must give a token to that player.

Make sure the players understand that everyone must tell the truth. You may also want to make some rules about good taste. For the most part, this game can challenge the young people to think creatively, and it will show them that everyone has missed doing something. The person who has missed the most in this game will end up taking home the most.

Wink and Wait

This is a popular game with young people. Everyone sits in a circle and faces the center. The leader must prepare a deck of playing cards that has only as many cards as there are players. It must include a joker. He or she lets everyone in the room take one card without showing it to anyone. Whoever draws the joker becomes the winker. No one, of course, knows who the winker is except the winker. Play begins with everyone looking around at one another and talking casually. The winker gets people out by *winking* at them. When a person notices that he or she has been winked at he or she *waits ten seconds* and then says "I'm out" and closes his or her eyes. The object is to guess who the winker is before being winked at. A person who guesses wrong is declared out. The winker tries to see how many people he or she can wink at before getting caught. When he or she is caught, the cards are collected and shuffled, and the game is replayed.

Match Up

Divide your group into two or more teams of equal number. Have each team choose a captain, who goes to the front of the room. Give everyone several slips of paper and a pencil. Ask the entire group a question, such as Who's going to win the World Series this year? Everyone, without any discussion, writes her or his answer on a slip of paper and passes it to the team captain, who has also written down an answer. The team captains announce their answers, and a point is awarded to each team for every answer that matches their team captain's. For example, if the team captain answered, "the Dodgers," his or her team gets a point for each answer that also was "the Dodgers." Here are some sample questions:

■ If you were going to repaint this room, what color would you paint it?
■ What country would you most like to visit?
■ What is your favorite TV show?
■ What is a number between one and five?
■ What book of the Bible says the most about good works?
■ What is the best way to have fun in this town?
■ What is the funniest word you can think of?
■ How many children do you want to have?

Map Game

For this game, get several identical state road maps. Draw a large number or letter on one map and make a list of all the towns that the figure crosses or comes near. Have the players divide into small groups and give each group an unmarked map and a copy of the list of towns. Tell the players that when you give the signal, they must locate the towns on the map and figure out what figure is formed when the towns on the list are connected with a line. A wrong guess by a group disqualifies that group. The first group to correctly identify the figure wins.

Mind Reading Games

In this series of games, at least two people know how the game is played. The object is for the group to figure out the "secret" that the mind reader and the leader are using to perform the trick. The person who thinks he or she knows the secret is allowed to test it. Each game can be played until most of the group has figured out the trick or until the secret is revealed.

   1. Black magic: While the mind reader is out of the room, the group picks any object in the room. The mind reader returns, and the leader points to many different objects. When he or she points to the chosen object, the mind reader correctly identifies it.
   The trick: The chosen object is pointed to immediately after a black object has been pointed to. The name of this game may help give it away, so give some thought to the feasibility of revealing the name.

   2. Book magic: Several books are placed in a row. One of them is chosen for the mind reader to guess when she or he returns to the room. The leader points to several books at random, and when she or he points to the correct book, the mind reader identifies it.
   The trick: The chosen book always follows any book pointed to that is on the end of the row.

3. Car: While the mind reader is out of the room, the group picks an object. The mind reader returns and is shown three objects. One of the three is the correct one. The mind reader correctly picks the chosen object.

The trick: The leader calls the mind reader back into the room with a statement that begins with either the letter *C, A,* or *R.* For example, "Come in," "All right," or "Ready." The letter *C* indicates the first object shown; the letter *A* represents the second object; the letter *R* signifies the third object. So when the mind reader comes back, he or she knows exactly which object will be the first, second, or third.

4. Knife, fork, and spoon game: In this game, the mind reader leaves the room and the group chooses one person to be the mystery person. Then the leader takes an ordinary knife, fork, and spoon and arranges them on the floor in some way. When the mind reader returns, she or he looks at the knife, the fork, and the spoon and correctly identifies the mystery person.

The trick: It actually has nothing at all to do with the knife, the fork, and the spoon. The leader uses them only as a diversionary tactic. After arranging the knife, the fork, and the spoon, the leader then takes a seat and sits in exactly the same position as the mystery person. If the mystery person is sitting cross-legged on the floor with one hand on his or her lap, the leader sits exactly the same way. If the mystery person changes position, so does the leader. The mind reader matches the leader's position and posture. Meanwhile, everyone is trying to figure out how the knife, the fork, and the spoon are giving away the clue.

5. Red, white, and blue: This is just like "Black Magic," only it is more confusing and almost impossible for the players to figure out.

The trick: The first time the mind reader tries to guess the chosen object, it immediately follows a red object. The next time, it follows a white object. The third time, it follows a blue object.

6. Smell the broom: The leader holds a broom horizontally in front of her or him, and someone in the group comes up and points to a particular spot on the broom handle. The mind reader enters the room and sniffs the handle until she or he finally stops at the correct spot. Everyone thinks that the mind reader has an incredible sense of smell.

The trick: While the mind reader is smelling the broom, she or he is really watching the leader's feet. As soon as the mind reader finds the correct spot on the broom handle, the leader raises her or his foot slightly so that it is undetected by the group.

7. Spirit move: In this game, the leader holds his or her hand over the head of a mystery person in the room while the mind reader, who is out of the room, is able to correctly identify that person.

The trick: Before the game begins, the leader and the mind reader agree on one special chair where the mystery person will sit. When the game begins, whoever is sitting in that chair will be the first one chosen. Both the leader and the mind reader note this person as instructions are being given to the group. The mind reader then leaves the room but remains within hearing distance. After everyone has moved to new seats, the leader calls to the mind reader and says "Spirit moves." He or she moves his or her hand over different people's heads until finally stopping over the head of the person who had been sitting in the special chair. The leader then says, "Spirit rests!" Calling out from his or her position outside the room, the mind reader identifies the mystery person to everyone's amazement. Then he or she enters the room to see if he or she named the correct person, but he or she is actually looking to see who is *now* in the special chair for the next round.

8. Writing in the sand: This one is a bit more complicated. The group selects a secret word and the mind reader guesses the word after a short series of clues from the leader. The leader holds a stick in her or his hand and appears to write the clues in the sand. The writing neither appears to make sense nor bears any obvious relationship to the secret word. But the mind reader is still able to guess the word on the first try.

The trick: Suppose the secret word is *light*. The consonants in the word are given to the mind reader through a series of verbal clues after he or she enters the room. The leader might first say, "Let's see if you can get this one." The first letter of that sentence is *l*. That would clue in the mind reader that the word starts with an *l*. Then the leader draws on the floor with the stick, and at some point taps out a number of taps, one through five. These taps represent the vowels. *A* is one tap; *e* is two taps, and so on. So in this example, the leader taps three times to signal the letter *i*. Now the mind reader has two letters. The *g* is given next with a verbal clue like, "Got it yet?" As soon as the mind reader has enough letters to guess the word, he or she amazes the group by identifying the word.

My Ship Sails

Have everyone sit but the leader, who begins the game by picking up a ball and saying, "My ship sails with . . . [naming something that begins with her or his initials]." For example, if the person's name is John Doe, he would say, "My ship sails with juicy donuts." He then throws the ball to another player in the room, and that player repeats "My ship sails with" and completes the sentence with some item. If the player does not know how to play, she or he will probably say something that does not begin with her or his initials. If so, she or he must stand up. That player remains standing until she or he catches on. When somebody throws the ball to her or him and she or he gets it right, she or he sits down. To start the game, at least two or three people need to know how to play. Explain at the beginning that not everybody's ship sails with the same things, and that the object is to discover the secret by listening to those who know.

How's Yours?

For this game, everyone is seated around the room, and a contestant is asked to leave. While that person is out, the group chooses a noun like *car* or *job,* which the contestant must guess. When the contestant returns, she or he asks, "How's yours?" to someone in the room. That person must respond with a true answer, describing the mystery noun. For example, if the noun is *car,* someone might respond with *old* or *expensive.* One-word adjectives are sufficient. The contestant tries to guess the noun after each adjective given. The last person to say an adjective before the correct noun is guessed becomes the new contestant.

Name That Place

This game is great for a small group divided into two teams or for a large group split into several teams. Find a book or a pamphlet that has pictures of a number of recognizable places in your city, or go on a photo spree and take some yourself. Make sure that you include a wide variety of photos—some that are easy to identify, like the city hall or the high school, and some that are difficult, like an unfamiliar perspective of a familiar landmark or a pond in a certain park or a tree on a street near the church.

Hold up each picture for the teams to see. The group that is first to correctly identify the spot wins a point. The team with the most points wins.

If your group is large, consider photocopying the pictures or projecting slides on a screen.

Rhythm

Everyone in the room numbers off in a circle. A rhythm is begun by number 1, and everyone joins in, by first slapping thighs, clapping hands, snapping right-hand fingers, then snapping left-hand fingers. Do it in a continuous 1-2-3-4-1-2-3-4-1-2-3-4 motion at a moderately slow speed, which may speed up after everyone learns how to play.

The real action begins when number 1 calls out his or her own number on the first snap of the fingers and calls out somebody else's number on the second snap of the fingers. The person with the second number called must follow suit, *in rhythm.* For example, it might sound something like this: slap, clap, *"One, six!"* Then number 6 might do slap, clap, *"Six, ten!"* Then number 10 would call out his or her number on the first snap and somebody else's number on the second, and so on. If anyone misses, he or she goes to the end of the numbered progression, and everybody who was after him or her before moves up one number. The object is to arrive at number 1's chair.

An interesting variation of this game is called "Symbol Rhythm." Instead of using numbers, each person uses a symbol like a cough, a whistle, or a scratch of the head. Rather than calling out numbers, each person does someone else's symbol—slap, clap, cough, scratch head. Still another version is "Animal Sound Rhythm," which substitutes animal sounds for numbers. Any way it is played, it is a lot of fun.

Open or Closed

The idea of this game is to learn a "secret." Have the young people sit in a circle and pass around a book or a pair of scissors. When the object is passed, each person announces how he or she received it and whether he or she is passing it open or closed. For example, he or she might say, "I received it open and I am passing it closed." The leader then informs the person whether he or she is right or wrong. If he or she is wrong, the leader tells him or her to sit (or stand elsewhere).

Continue until everyone is disqualified or until the players figure out the secret.

The trick: If the leader's legs are *crossed,* the young person must pass the object *closed.* If the leader's legs are *uncrossed,* the player must pass the object *open.* It sounds simple, but it really is hard to figure out, which makes for a fun game.

S and T

Divide the group in half. Name one side the "S and T" group and the other side the "Everyone Else" group. Have both groups count together from one to twenty. Tell the groups that every time they say a number that begins with an *S* or a *T,* the "S and T" group is to stand up, and when they say all the other numbers, the "Everyone Else" group is to stand up. Start slowly, then repeat the numbers a little faster. The faster you count, the better the game.

To vary this game, have everyone sit in a circle and count off up to twenty. If you have more than twenty players, begin at one again. Every time a person says a number that begins with an *S* or a *T,* he or she must stand up before saying it. Any player who does not is out, and the game continues. The counting must be done in rhythm without waiting. It is confusing, but lots of fun.

The Situation Game

If your group is sitting in a circle or in rows of chairs, this game will liven things up. Have everyone whisper the name of a person to the person on their right, for example, "You are _____ [Batman, Brigitte Bardot, etc.]." Urge them to be creative. Then have everyone whisper a location to the person on their left, for example, "You are _____ [in the bathtub, on top of a flagpole, etc.]." Next ask everybody to find a new seat. Then have them whisper to the person on their right, "You are wearing _____." To the person on their left, "You are doing

_____ ." Ask each person to tell the group who she or he is, where she or he is, what she or he is wearing, and what she or he is doing. The results are hilarious.

Third Degree

Divide the group into two teams, one composed of FBI members, the other of spies. Each spy is given a card with one of the instructions listed here (keep a record of what each spy's assignment is). The FBI members take turns asking questions of specific spies, calling out the name of each spy before asking the question. They may ask as many questions of as many spies as they choose. Each spy must answer each question but only in the manner described on her or his card. Whenever a spy's instruction is guessed correctly by an FBI member, she or he is eliminated. The questions continue until all the spies' instructions are guessed correctly. If a spy gives an answer without following her or his instructions, she or he is eliminated. An FBI member can make a guess at any time.

The winning spy is the one who has the most questions asked before her or his instructions are guessed correctly. The winning FBI member is the one who correctly guesses the most instructions.

1. Lie during every answer.
2. Answer each question as though you were _____ [the name of an adult leader].
3. Try to start an argument with each answer you give.
4. Always name some color in your answers.
5. Always use a number in your answers.
6. Be evasive—never actually answer a question.
7. Always answer a question with a question.
8. Always exaggerate your answers.
9. Always pretend to misunderstand the question by your answer.
10. Always scratch during your answers.
11. Always begin each answer with a cough.
12. Always mention some kind of food during each answer.
13. Always mention the name of a group member during your answers.

A variation on this game is to give everyone an instruction like those listed previously. Then have each person answer questions from the entire group until someone can guess her or his secret instruction. Each new question asked without the instruction being guessed is worth a point.

Statistical Treasure Hunt

This exceptionally good game gets groups acquainted. Divide your group into teams of equal number, if possible. Give each team a pencil and a copy of this game sheet. These questions may suggest other questions to you that may be more appropriate for your particular group or occasion. Have each team appoint a captain who acts as the gleaner of information and the recorder. Set a time limit. The team with the highest score wins.

Statistical Treasure Hunt

_____ 1. Counting January as one point, February as two points, and so on, through the calendar year, total the number of birthday points at your table—use months not years.

_____ 2. Counting one point for each different state named, total the score for the different number of birth states represented.

_____ 3. Total all the shoe sizes—one foot only.

_____ 4. Total the number of operations everyone at your table has had. Serious dental surgery counts, but not just an ordinary tooth pulling. Save all the interesting details for later!

_____ 5. Total your hair color score: black counts two; brown counts one; blond counts three; red counts five.

_____ 6. Score a point for each self-made article worn or carried by your teammates.

_____ 7. Add the total number of miles traveled by each member to get to this meeting.

_____ 8. Score one point for each different high school attended.

Permission to reproduce this page for use with your group is granted.

Taking a Trip

This memory game is always fun. Everyone sits in a circle, and the leader begins by saying, "I'm taking a trip, and I'm bringing _____ [anything can be named]." The second person then says, "I'm taking a trip, and I'm bringing _____ [the item named by the first person] and _____ [a new item]." Continuing around the circle, each person names all the items that have already been mentioned, plus his or her own addition. This continues until someone makes a mistake. Whoever remembers the most items in the correct order wins.

Dictionary

Dictionary can be played by any number of people. All that is needed is a dictionary, pencils, and three-by-five-inch index cards. One person finds a word in the dictionary that she or he thinks no one will know the definition of. She or he asks the group to make sure that no one knows the definition. She or he then copies the correct definition on an index card. Everyone else also writes a definition of the word on an index card and signs it.

The definitions are collected and read to the group, along with the correct one. The object is to guess the correct one. A point is given to each participant who guesses the right definition. A point is also given to each participant for every person who thinks her or his wrong definition is correct. The person choosing the original word is given five points if no one guesses the correct answer.

The first person to choose the correct definition gets to select the next word. If no one guesses correctly, the person who chose the word goes again.

Who Am I?

This oldie but goodie is always a lot of fun. On slips of paper, write different names of famous people and pin them to the back of each person, not letting anyone see the name that was pinned on them. Each person is to ask other group members questions that can be answered either yes or no to help him or her guess who he or she is. The players may only ask one question per person. The first person to guess correctly is the winner; however, the game should continue until everyone has guessed their identity.

True-False Scramble

Here is a good game to test Bible knowledge. Two teams sit in opposite rows of chairs and number off. At one end of the rows is the True Chair, at the other is the False Chair. The leader makes a statement based on a biblical passage. It can be a false statement, such as "The lunch Jesus used to feed more than five thousand people was five hamburgers and two Cokes," or a true one, such as "Jesus said, 'I am the way, the truth, and the life.'" After the statement, the leader calls out some numbers. The players with those numbers race for what they believe to be the correct chair. The first one there wins a point for her or his team. When the players return to their seat, the leader says the correct answer. The team that answers the most questions correctly wins.

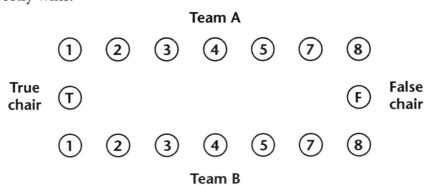

Name That Scripture

This game can be used at a youth meeting or at a youth group social to test your group's knowledge of familiar biblical passages.

Divide your group into two teams. Have the two teams position themselves on opposite sides of the room and position yourself in the middle. Be prepared with a list of well-known biblical verses of about ten to twelve words each.

Ask each team to select one person to compete in the first round. Have the players bid on the number of words within which they think they can guess the verse, for example, "I can name that verse in six words" or "I can name that verse in five words." The bidding continues until one player stops. If the winning bid is two words, say the first two words of the verse. And the player who bid two words must finish the verse correctly. If he or she is successful, the team gets a point. If unsuccessful, the opposing player gets an additional word and the opportunity to complete the verse. If successful, he or she gets the point. If the second player does not complete the verse correctly, the first player tries again with an additional word, and so on.

To make the game a bit more risky, lay down the following rule: If you win the bid and cannot complete the verse correctly, the opposing player gets two points if he or she says it correctly.

To make the game even riskier, tell the teams that the second player may consult with his or her team. This ensures that the bidding is taken seriously. It is a lot of fun and is educational, too!

Password

Password works well for small youth-group meetings. Here is how it is played: You need two teams of two. Ahead of time, select a number of words to be guessed and write them on three-by-five-inch cards. Any words will do, but nouns are generally best. After deciding which team will go first, show the same secret word to player *A* on each team. Have player *A* on the starting team give a one-word clue to her or his partner and direct the partner (player *B*) to try to guess the correct word. If she or he misses, the other team gets a chance. If that team also misses, the first team tries again, and so on. This is the best seating arrangement:

A ☐   ☐ A

☐
Leader
B ☐   ☐ B

Players face each other.

Here is the scoring system:
- five points for a correct guess on the first clue
- four points for a correct guess on the second clue
- three points for a correct guess on the third clue
- two points for a correct guess on the fourth clue
- one point for a correct guess on the fifth clue

Give up if no one has guessed correctly after the fifth clue and go on to the next word. The game ends when one team reaches twenty-one or any score chosen ahead of time.

The game can also be played with the entire group at once. For example, if you have eight players on each team, use this seating:

A ☐ ☐ ☐ ☐   ☐ ☐ ☐ ☐ A

☐
Leader

B ☐ ☐ ☐ ☐   ☐ ☐ ☐ ☐ B

Team 1   **Team 2**

Write each mystery word on a large card and hold it up so that all the player *A*'s can see it, but not the player *B*'s. The first player *A* in each line gives the first clue to the player sitting across from him or her. If both player *B*'s are unsuccessful, they move to the end of their line and a new person on each team tries for the correct answer. Other rules stay the same. Alternate each time so that player *A* is the clue giver in one round and player *B* is the clue giver in the next round.

PART 3

Indoor Action Games

Introduction

The games in this section are best played indoors in a gymnasium or a recreation room. Unlike the games in the first two sections, these games involve a good deal of physical activity and movement. Keep in mind that many of them can also be adapted for play outdoors. As you plan the games, be sure to check that boundaries are or can be clearly marked and that furniture and fixtures that might easily break are removed, secured, or covered. If your space is not quite adequate to the game at hand, give some thought to creatively adapting the rules or to shrinking or expanding the boundaries to fit your situation. A good deal of fun can be squeezed out of less-than-ideal situations. Try to see an abbreviated playing field as a challenge rather than a hurdle.

Clothespin Challenge

This is a simple game for teams of two. Pairs are seated in chairs facing each other with their knees touching. Each player is shown a large pile of clothespins at the right of his or her chair. Each player is blindfolded and given two minutes to pin as many clothespins as possible onto the pant legs of the other contestant.

Alphabet Pong

For this game, the group arranges itself into a circle. Each person holds a book with both hands. One player uses a book to hit a Ping-Pong ball across the circle and calls "*A.*" The person on the other side then returns it calling out "*B,*" and so forth. The circle works together to see how far through the alphabet it can get before it misses, that is, allows the ball to hit the floor. There is no particular order for hitting the ball. Anyone can hit it when it comes to her or him, but no one may hit the ball twice in a row. Adapt this game to teams by having the first team play and then the other team. The winning team is the one that gets the furthest through the alphabet without the ball hitting the floor. It is a real challenge!

Back Snatching

Pin a name onto each person's back. Announce a time limit. Direct the players to copy the names of the other players and at the same time to keep others from copying the name on their back. Expect a lot of twisting and turning. The player with the most names is the winner.

Back-to-Back

Divide your group into pairs and have them sit on the floor back-to-back and link arms. Then tell them to stand up. With a little timing and cooperation, this should not be too hard. Next direct the pair to join another pair and create a foursome. Have the foursome sit on the floor back-to-back with arms linked. Tell them to stand up. This will be more difficult. Keep adding more people to the group until the giant blob cannot stand up any more.

Balloon Golf

This game is good in a small game room and outdoors when there is no wind. First, drop a penny or a smooth stone into each round balloon. Then blow the balloon up so it is about five or six inches in diameter. (When the balloon is inflated, the weight inside creates a Mexican-jumping-bean effect, causing both difficulty and hilarity for the participants.) Make golf clubs by rolling a full sheet of newspaper into a stick. Use cardboard boxes as the holes and label the par for each hole on the side of the box.

Balloon Burst

Divide your group into two teams and pick a captain for each. Arrange them as diagrammed below. Toss a balloon between the rows. Each team tries to hit the balloon in the direction of its captain, who will then burst the balloon with a pin. Keep the game going as long as you want by tossing in balloons one at a time. One point is scored for each balloon burst. Players must stay seated and use only one hand.

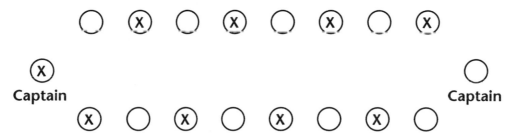

Bubble Head

For this simple game, people pair off and stand facing each other about four feet apart. For each pair, blow up a round balloon and have one player bump the balloon off her or his head to the other player and the second player bounce the balloon off her or his head back to the first player.

The balloon must be hit with the head only. The distance between players can be adjusted for greater or lesser difficulty. Each player can move only the left foot while attempting to hit the balloon. No jumping is allowed, although each player is allowed to pivot on the ball of his or her right foot. The object is to see how many times the pairs can bounce the balloon without dropping it.

A variation on this game is to have the pairs line up facing each other about four feet apart, creating two opposing teams. Each team must bounce a balloon all the way down the team line from one head to the other. Again, right feet must remain planted. If a balloon is dropped, the team must start over again. The first team to succeed is the winner.

Bite the Bag

Stand a grocery bag in the middle of the floor and ask everyone to sit in a wide circle around it. Ask each person to come to the bag, try to pick it up with his or her teeth, and return to a standing position. Nothing but the bottoms of his or her feet are allowed to touch the floor. Almost everyone can do this. After everyone has had a turn, cut off or fold down the bag an inch or two. Again have each person come forward as before. With each round, shorten the bag more. When a person is no longer able to pick up the bag and stand again, he or she is out. The winner is the one who can pick up the bag without falling.

Church Trivia

Divide the group into teams or let the young people compete individually. Give each a list of easily overlooked or unusual things in the church to identify. Here is a sample list:
1. the name of the company that manufactured the church's fire extinguisher
2. the number of steps to the altar
3. the number of fuses (or circuit breakers) in the fuse box
4. the location of the first-aid kit
5. the last word in a particular book in the church library
6. the number of yellow lines painted on the parking lot

Your list should include twenty or more items such as these. On "go," turn everyone loose to try to gather the information as quickly as possible. With teams, assign the questions to different members. The first team to finish answering the most questions correctly wins.

Clothespinning

Here is a wild game that is simple yet fun to play with any size group. Give everyone in the group six clothespins. On the signal "go," each player tries to pin one clothespin on other players' clothing. Each person's clothespins must be attached to six different players. The players must keep moving to avoid being "clothespinned" while trying to hang their clothespins on someone else. When a player hangs all six clothespins, he or she is to remain in the game but try to avoid getting any more clothespins. At the end of a time limit, the person with the least amount of clothespins is the winner.

Another way to play this game is to divide the group into pairs and give each person six clothespins. Each person then tries to hang all the pins on his or her partner. When the whistle is blown, the player with the least number of pins is the winner. The winners continue to pair off until there is a champion clothespinner.

Comic Strip Mixer

Find a Sunday-paper comic strip that has as many frames as you have small-group members. Cut the frames apart and pin one on the back of each person in the group. (You could, for example, make a ten-frame comic work for an eight-member team by giving two people each a piece made up of two frames.) Have the young people try to

arrange themselves in the correct order, so that the comic strip makes sense. Since the frames are on the players' backs, they must communicate with one another to accomplish this task.

For larger groups, use several different comic strips (preferably ones that have the same number of frames) and pin them randomly on everyone's back. The winning team is the first one to line up with a completed comic strip in its correct order.

Indoor Volleyball

You can play an exciting volleyball game inside, even with a low ceiling, by using a Nerf basketball. If you do not have a regular net, rig one up by draping sheets across a taut rope or stack tables between the teams. For low ceilings, keep the net low and have everyone play while sitting or kneeling on the floor. Other volleyball rules apply.

Down the Drain

For this game, you will need the type of plastic tube used to protect the clubs in a golf bag. You can probably borrow these from someone because the game will not damage them.

Divide the group into two equal teams. Give each team half the tubes or one for each player. Have the players line up side-by-side with their team members. Direct them to hold the tubes end-to-end, using their hands to secure the joints.

Have a leader from each team simultaneously place a marble in the end of his or her team's first tube. The object is for the teams to move the marble down all the tubes and out the other end. The team that is first to do this is the winner. If the marble slips through one of the joints and falls onto the floor, the team is disqualified. Once the players get the hang of it, they should be able to do this rather smoothly. Some strategy is involved, however, and they will enjoy the challenge.

To make the game a little longer, set up a series, declaring the team with the best two out of three to be the winner, or give each team ten marbles to send "down the drain." Only one marble is allowed in the drain at a time. Ask somebody to catch the marbles when they come out.

Electric Fence

For this game, a fence is created by tying a rope about two feet off the floor between two poles.

This game also needs two teams that are evenly divided according to height, age, and sex. The object of the game is for the entire team to get over the electric fence (the rope) without getting electro-cuted (touching the rope). Each team takes a turn, with team members going one at a time.

After each successful try, the rope is raised a little higher. Though one player at a time goes over the rope, the other team members can help any way they want. However, once a person is over the fence, she or he must stay on the other side and may not return. The last person must somehow get over the fence without help on one side. This game requires lots of teamwork and cooperation.

Teams can be eliminated entirely if one person touches the fence, but as the rope gets higher and higher, consider eliminating individual members.

Cup It

This game should be played in a room without carpeting. Two equal teams are needed. Team *A* throws first and sits behind home plate. Team *B*, which is in the field, scatters around the room. Each fielding team member is given a paper cup.

A player from Team *A* throws a Ping-Pong ball into the field from no lower than shoulder height. Team *B* players attempt to catch the ball with a paper cup in as few bounces as possible. Team *A* receives a point for each time the ball bounces on the floor before being cupped. A maximum of fifteen bounces is allowed. Referees should be appointed to keep track of the bounces. Each member of the team gets one throw, and then the other team comes up. The points scored are totaled at the close of every inning. Play as many innings as time will allow. Here are additional rules:

- *Out-of-bounds:* Draw lines across home plate and open doorways. The ball must not be thrown behind the plate or through doorways. A throw that hits low hanging lights is considered an out.
- *Throwing:* Throwing may be in any direction, but when the ball is released, the hand must be above the plane of the thrower's shoulder. Fielders may not stand directly in front of the thrower or hinder the thrower in any way.

Inversion

This game requires teamwork. Draw two parallel lines on the floor about eighteen inches apart. Ask the group to line up inside the parallel lines and number off. At a signal, tell the players that they must reverse their number order without stepping outside the parallel lines. For example, if fourteen people are in the group, player 1 must change places with player 14, and so on. If you have an odd-numbered group, only the person in the middle stays in the same place.

Let the group practice this and develop a strategy for doing it quickly and accurately. Then have them compete against the clock to set a world record for the youth group. Or if you have teams, see which team can reassemble most quickly. Consider appointing referees to penalize a team in seconds lost whenever a player steps outside one of the lines, or you can assume this role yourself.

Flea Market

Ahead of time, cut a large number of one-inch-square pieces of paper of different colors. Write the numbers 7, 11, 13, and 15 on some of them. Hide these around the room. At a starting signal, have the group hunt for the squares. Explain that as soon as they have found the squares, they can start trading them with one another, trying to acquire the colors and the numbered pieces that they think are worth the most. Point out that the value of the colors and the numbers will remain unknown to them until the trading is over. After the trading is over, announce the values. The person who has the most points wins. This game can also be adapted into an Easter egg hunt. Here is the scoring system:

Colors
- white = one point
- brown = five points
- green = subtract five points
- blue = two points
- red = ten points

Numbers
- 7 = fifty
- 11 = double the score
- 13 = subtract fifty
- 15 = one

Human Tic-Tac-Toe

As suggested by its title, this game has the same object as regular tic-tac-toe except that people are used. It is active and great for small groups. Nine chairs are set in three rows of three. Team *A* stands on one side of the chairs, and team *B* on the other. Players on each team then number off.

The leader calls a number and the two players with that number scramble to sit down in any chair as quickly as they can. When they are seated, another number is called, and play continues until three teammates from either team have successfully lined themselves in a row of three, either vertically, horizontally, or diagonally. If no team has done so, the players return to their team, and the game is played again.

A variation of this would be to play with ten people per game (five on a team). They all take a seat in one of the nine chairs, leaving one person without a seat. When the whistle is blown, everyone must get up and move to a different chair, while the extra person tries to sit down somewhere. After the mad scramble for seats, the game is scored like tic-tac-toe. Any row of three people from the same team gets points. In each round, one person will always be left without a seat.

An even crazier variation is to play as described above, but use people on their hands and knees as chairs. When the whistle is blown, the people on the "chairs" jump up and grab another chair. They must hang on because other players may try to pull them off or take the same person. It is really wild.

Whether you use chairs, people, lines on the floor, or whatever, Human Tic-Tac-Toe is a lot of fun.

Long John Stuff

This hilarious game is always fun with any group. Get two pairs of long underwear, a straight pin, and about one hundred small, round balloons. Divide the group into two teams. Have each team select one person to wear the long johns. The long johns should comfortably fit over the players' regular clothes. Have each team also select two or three balloon stuffers.

When the players are ready, throw out an equal number of balloons to each team. Tell the team members that they must blow up the balloons, tie them, and pass them to the stuffers who try to stuff them into the long johns. Advise the teams that they have two minutes to see which team can stuff the most balloons into their person's long johns. Call time and have the balloon stuffers stop. To count the balloons, begin with the one who appears to have the fewest balloons and pop them with a pin (through the long johns) while the team counts. (Be careful that you do not stick the contestant with the pin).

Mad Hatter

This free-for-all is really wild. Give everybody a hat (use ski caps if you want the game to last longer). Give everybody a club—a sock stuffed full of cloth or something soft. At a signal, the players are to attempt to knock off everybody else's cap while keeping on their own. They may not use their hands to protect themselves or to keep their cap on, and they may not knock off anyone's cap with anything except the sock club. Those who lose their cap are out of the game.

Indoor Soccer

For this game, create two teams of no more than five or six players on each team and set up or mark a goal at each end of the room. Place a feather or a Ping-Pong ball between the two teams. Clear an open space on the floor, and have all the players get down on their hands and knees. Have the players try to *blow* the feather or the Ping-Pong ball across the other teams's goal line. No hands are allowed.

Musical Backs

This is similar to musical chairs and other elimination games. The young people mill about the room, and when the music stops or the whistle blows, everyone must quickly find another person and stand back-to-back. When an odd number of people are playing, someone will not have a partner, and she or he is eliminated. When there is an even number of people playing, a chair is placed in their midst, and anyone may sit in it and be safe. Every other round, the chair will need to be removed. Everyone must keep moving, and players may not pair off with the same person twice in a row. It's a lot of fun.

Musical Costumes

This game allows everyone to look a little silly. Before you start, collect a laundry bag or a pillowcase full of various articles of outer clothing—funny hats, baggy pants, gloves, belts. Try to have enough so that each person can get three or four funny articles of clothing. This game can lend itself to seasonal themes, such as Santa's bag or an Easter parade. This game can also be a fun way to create an instant costume for a Halloween party.

Have your group form a circle and start passing the bag around as music is played. Keep the bag tied shut as it is passed so that the clothing does not spill out. When you stop the music, direct the person holding the bag to unfasten it, reach in, and take out an article without looking. Have him or her put the article on and wear it for the remainder of the game. After the game, you can have a fashion show or take pictures to display on a bulletin board.

Paper Shoot

Divide the group into teams of four to eight players each. In the middle of the room, set a garbage can on a chair or a table so that it is about three feet off the floor. Make several paper batons and a lot of wadded-up paper balls. Have the members of one team lie down on their back around the trash can with their head toward it. Give each of these players a paper baton. Position the opposing team around the trash can behind a line about ten feet or so away from it. Tell the players that the task of the standing team is to throw the wadded-up paper balls into the can and that the other team's task is to knock the balls away with their batons while lying on their backs. Announce that the standing team has two minutes to shoot as many paper balls into the can as possible. After each team has had its chance to be in both positions, the team that got the most paper balls in the can wins. To make the game a bit more difficult for the throwers, have them sit in chairs.

Musical Hats

Pick any number of players to stand in a circle, each facing the back of the player next to her or him. All should be facing clockwise or all counterclockwise. Provide hats for all the players except one. Explain that when the music starts (or at a signal), each player should grab the hat off the head of the person in front of her or him and put it on her or his own head, continuing to do so until the music stops. Tell the players that when the music stops (or a signal is given), the player who is left without a hat is out of the game. Remove one hat after each round and continue the game until only two players are left. To pick a winner, have the pair stand back-to-back and direct them to grab the single hat off each other's head. When the music stops, the one wearing the hat wins.

Nerfketball

Here is a fun variation of basketball using a Nerf basketball or a soft sponge and a few chairs. Choose two teams of equal number and seat them alternately on sturdy chairs as shown in the diagram: two rows of players facing each other. For best results, players should be spaced at least double arm's distance apart both sideways and across. Place a small bucket for the basket on the floor at the end of each double row, approximately six feet from the players at the ends of the rows.

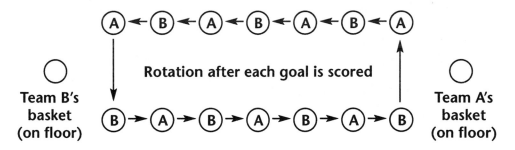

Here are the two ground rules:
- Chairs cannot be moved or tipped.
- Each player must remain seated while the ball is in play.

Flip a coin to decide which team will take first possession of the ball. Play begins when the referee gives the ball to the player farthest from his or her team's goal. The team tries to work the ball toward its goal by passing it while opponents try to block passes and steal the ball. Any player may take a shot at the goal at any time, but the advantage of passing the ball to the player nearest the goal is obvious. If the ball is intercepted by the other team, play continues in the opposite direction.

When a field goal attempt misses, the ball goes to the other team, and play goes the other way. When a field goal is scored, all players rotate one seat to the right. This will give all players the opportunity to be their team's prime shooter during the game. After rotation, the ball goes to the other team.

Any ball loose within the playing area is a free ball. Any ball going outside the playing area is given to the player nearest the last player to touch the ball.

Penalties may be assessed. When players leave their seat or show unnecessary roughness, award free throws to the other team. Limit the game either by using a kitchen timer for quarters and halves or by setting a scoring limit.

Sanctuary Soccer

This version of soccer allows you to play indoors and has a built-in equalizer to keep one team from dominating the game.

Play in a large room that is obstacle-free. You will need a Nerf soccer ball or any soft ball and eight folding chairs. Line up four chairs at each end of the playing area for goals. The game follows regular soccer rules, but as many players as you wish can play. A team scores when the ball hits one of the other team's chairs. The chair that is hit is removed from the goal of the team that was scored upon and added to the goal of the team that scored. For example, before the first goal is scored, the setup would look like this:

Team A's goal □ □ Team B's goal

Diagram A

After team *B* scores, the setup would look like this:

Team A's goal □ □ Team B's goal

Diagram B

The team that was just scored upon will have an easier, larger target when the ball is back in play, while the other team has a smaller, more difficult target.

Ping-Pong Basketball

This game can be played individually or in teams but is best played on a hard floor. It is simple and fun. Set up a large number of different-size containers around the room and assign each one a point value. The larger the container, the lower the point value. Then have the players try to bounce Ping-Pong balls into the containers for points. The ball must bounce at least once before it goes into a container.

Ping-Pong Variations

Ping-Pong is an old standby for small youth groups, but these interesting versions of the game can make it even more challenging.

1. Round table Ping-Pong: As many as twenty persons may play this variation. One person picks up a paddle at each end of the table. Other players line up clockwise and a little behind these two players. One person serves, drops the paddle on the table, and moves around the table clockwise as the next person picks up the paddle and returns the ball. Rotation continues until someone misses. The player who misses is out of the game.

2. Spool pong: This is played like regular Ping-Pong, except that it requires two spools, one placed on each side of the net, on the center line of the table about eighteen inches from the ends of the table. An extra Ping-Pong ball is placed on top of each spool. Five points are added to the score if the opponent's ball is knocked off the spool. Otherwise the game is scored normally.

3. Water pong: Two small saucers filled with water are placed one on each side of the net about twelve inches from the net and on the center line. If one player hits the ball into the other's saucer, he or she wins the game. Otherwise, the game is scored normally.

Pinball Soccer

Here is a new way to play soccer indoors. It is just like regular soccer, except that each person, including the goalie, must stand on a piece of paper. The players must keep one foot on the paper at all times. Scooting the paper is not allowed. The players of both teams must be evenly scattered over the entire playing area. The game begins when a soccer ball is tossed to the middle of the floor. Watch the fun. The effect is like watching a giant pinball machine.

Shuffle Your Buns

Here is a fun game you can play over and over again. Arrange chairs— one per player—in a circle. Two people stand in the middle. The rest sit in chairs. The people in the middle must try to sit down, while the seated people try to keep them from doing so by moving from chair to chair. When a player in the middle manages to sit in a chair, the person on her or his right goes to the middle.

Fickle Feather

Lay a sheet flat on the floor. All the players kneel around all four sides of the sheet and pick it up by the edges. They pull it taut and hold it under their chin. A feather is placed on the sheet, and the young people try to blow it away from their side. The players on each side of the sheet are a team. If the feather touches one of the team members or gets blown over a team member's head, that team gets a point. The team with the fewest points is the winner.

Snow Fight

This game creates quite a mess, but it's worth it. Divide into two teams and put a divider (e.g., a couple rows of chairs, back-to-back) down the center of the room. Place the two teams on opposite sides of the divider. Give each team a large stack of old newspapers, then give them five or ten minutes to prepare their "snow" by wadding the paper into balls—the more, the better. Caution: Beforehand, check to see if the newspaper ink easily rubs off on hands and clothes. If it does, use old magazines for this activity—or you will have irate parents!

Tell the teams that when the signal to begin is given, they are to start tossing snow at the opposing team. This really does look like a snowstorm. Also tell them that when the whistle blows, everyone must stop throwing. Determine the winner by deciding which team has the least amount of snow on its side of the divider.

Have players who are at risk of losing their eyeglasses or other personal belongings set them aside or secure them in some way. The snow can get pretty deep. After the game is over, provide plastic garbage bags and have a race to see which side can stuff its snow into the bags first.

Technicolor Stomp

This indoor game is really wild. You will need a lot of colored balloons. Divide into teams and assign each team a color. Then give each team an equal number of balloons in their color. Have the players blow up and tie all the balloons. Release the balloons onto the floor. Tell the teams that the object is to stomp on and pop all the balloons of the *other* teams while attempting to protect their own team's balloons. When everyone is ready, shout "Go!" After two or three minutes, blow a whistle to signal the end of the game. Have each team gather up its remaining balloons. The team with the most balloons is the winner.

Steal the Bacon

This is an old favorite. Divide your group into two teams and line up the teams facing each other behind two lines (twenty to thirty feet apart). Have each team number off from left to right. This way, no one will be facing an opponent with the same number. Place a handkerchief or a towel in the center, at a point equidistant from both teams.

Call a number. The player on each team having that number tries to snatch the handkerchief and return to her or his place without being tagged by the other player. The more skilled players will run into the center and hover over the handkerchief until she or he can snatch it and run when her or his opponent is off guard. Each successful return gains one point for the team. After each successful tag or score, the handkerchief is returned to the center, and another number is called. Play for a designated number of points. The leader should call numbers in a way that builds suspense. All numbers should be included, but repeat a number now and then to keep all the players alert. Also maintain interest by calling two or more numbers simultaneously.

Chair Ball

This exciting version of basketball can be played on any open field or in a large room. A ball that is a bit lighter, like a playground ball or a Nerf ball, works best. Any number of people can be on a team. A person standing on a chair and holding a wastebasket or a similar container is positioned at each end of the playing area. A jump ball starts the game, as in basketball. The players try to move the ball down the field to shoot a basket. The person on the chair, who is holding the basket, may try to help by moving the basket to catch the ball when it is shot. All shots must be made behind a ten-foot foul line. The ball may only be moved downfield by throwing it to a teammate or by kicking it. Players may not run or walk with the ball. Points are scored using the basketball scoring system.

Triple Threat Basketball

Here is a crazy way to play basketball. It requires one basket and three teams of any size; however, a maximum of five players or a minimum of two is best. The rules of the game are similar to regular basketball, but with these changes:

■ Baskets are worth one point. The game is played until one team has ten points and is leading the other two teams by at least two points each.

■ After each basket is scored, the team in last place is awarded the ball out of bounds, even if it was the team that last scored. In the event that more than one team is tied for last, the team that has had the low point total the longest is awarded the ball.

- In the event that play is stopped for some reason other than a basket, such as the ball going out-of-bounds, or a player traveling or double dribbling, the team in last place is again awarded the ball. If the last-place team is guilty of the violation, the ball is given to the team that is next-to-last.
- In the event of a foul, the team that was fouled takes the ball out-of-bounds. There are no foul shots.

   This game can be played with two baskets on a regular basketball court. Teams rotate baskets after each goal is scored. Another version is to play with four teams and four baskets, one of each on each side of a square, if the baskets are movable. Also, the game can be played with a Nerf ball and cardboard boxes or trash cans for baskets. Be creative and have fun!

Towel Throw

For this game, the group is seated in chairs, preferably in a closed circle. One person stands inside the circle. The group passes or throws a towel around the circle to anyone in the circle. The person in the middle then tries to tag the person who has the towel. When she or he catches somebody with the towel, they exchange positions. If she or he catches the towel in midair, the person who threw it has to trade places with the person in the middle.

Trash Can Basketball

This version of basketball can be played when a court is not available. Set up large trash cans at each end of the room. Use a Nerf ball or some other type of soft ball. Follow regular basketball rules with these exceptions:
- No dribbling is allowed. All movement of the ball is by passing. This helps to make the game not only more practical but fairer.
- No running with the ball is allowed, only passing to a teammate.
- If a player is touched with the ball, it is a foul. The fouled player gets a free shot.
- Draw a circle around each trash can about six feet out. The area inside the circles is out-of-bounds, and no one is allowed here. This prevents goaltending and dunking, making the game fairer for everyone.

Bean Blitz

This is a good way to get young people involved with one another at the beginning of a meeting or a social event. Each player is given an envelope containing twenty beans. The players wander around the room holding in their closed hands a few beans from the envelope. They approach other people, one at a time, and ask, "Odd or even?" referring to the beans in their hand. The players who guess correctly get the beans. The players who guess wrong must give up the same number of beans. (The guesser is required to guess *only whether the number is odd or even,* not what the actual number of beans is.) A time limit is set, and whoever has the most beans at the end wins a prize. When a player's beans are gone, he or she is out.

Underdog

This game should be played in a large, open space. Choose one player to be "It." This person's role is to tag the other players, who in turn must freeze when they are tagged. Frozen players may be unfrozen by standing with their legs apart and allowing a free player to go between them. The person who is It tries to freeze all the free players, and when he or she does, the game is over. For larger groups, make several players It at the same time.

Rainbow Soccer

This active game is played with two teams and sixty balloons (thirty each of two colors). The balloons are mixed together and placed in the center circle of a regulation basketball court. Assign a balloon color to each team. The two teams line up on the end lines facing each other. One person from each team is the goalie and stands in front of a large container at the opposite end of the floor from her or his team.

At the whistle, each team (using soccer rules) tries to kick its balloons to its goalie, who then puts the balloons into the container behind her or him. To play defense, a team stomps and pops as many of the other team's balloons as possible. Play continues until all the balloons are popped or are in a container. The team with the most goals wins.

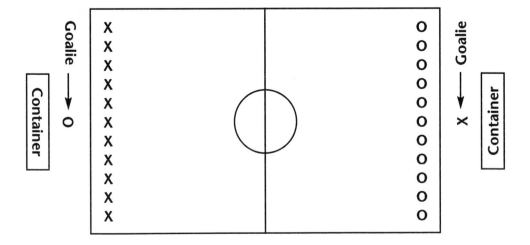

PART 4

Outdoor Action Games

Introduction

All the games in this section are best played outdoors on an open field, in someone's backyard, or at a camp or a retreat. For more outdoor games, use any of the relays suggested in part 5, "Relays and Races." As in other games, these games require no more than the usual equipment that most school and church groups possess, such as specialized and relatively inexpensive equipment for regular volleyball, soccer, softball, basketball, baseball, and football. The games in this section take liberties with the normal rules of these familiar games, and the crazy variations make them fun and reduce the tension that often arises when players think that they must win. In these games, the players are invited to have fun and be a little weird.

Scat

Here is an old game that is probably new for most of your group. To play, you need a volleyball or playground ball. Assign everyone a number. Decide on two mystery numbers that are not assigned to anyone. No one knows what the mystery numbers are except you. As you throw the ball up in the air, call out a number. Everyone scatters except the person whose number is called. That person immediately retrieves the ball and yells "Stop!" All the other players must then freeze in their tracks. The person tries to hit someone with the ball. If hit, the player gets a letter (*S, C, A,* or *T*), but if the throw misses, the thrower gets a letter. If a mystery number is called, then everyone automatically gets a letter. The two mystery numbers may be called only once. People who get the four letters *S-C-A-T* are eliminated.

Bucket Brigade

You need two teams for this game. Direct each team to line up single file with a bucket of water on one end and an empty bucket on the other. Give each team member a paper cup and explain that the object of the game is to transfer the water from one bucket to the other by pouring the water from cup to cup down the line. The first team to get all its water to the empty bucket is the winner.

Crazy Baseball

This version of baseball can be played with any size group by changing the foul lines, moving them closer together for small groups or farther apart for large groups.

Divide the young people into two teams. Use a partly deflated volleyball and a baseball bat. Use two bases—home plate and first base. First base can be any distance away from home plate. The team at bat selects a member of its team to pitch. Batters only get one pitch, and they must swing. If they miss the ball entirely, they are out. Two foul balls or a fly ball that is caught constitute an out. As soon as the ball is hit, the batter runs to first base. The fielding team can get a force out at first or hit the runner with the ball.

When the batter gets to first base, she or he does not have to come home until it is safe to do so. In other words, the team at bat can have five or six people on first base at the same time. Then when a ball is well hit, all five people can score a run at once by running for home plate.

The fielding team can play all over the field. The only designated positions are first baseman and catcher. As soon as the batting team gets three outs, the team in the field can run immediately up to home plate and start hitting. They do not have to wait for the other team to get ready in the field.

Batters should line up at home plate boy-girl-boy-girl and number off so they can get in the same batting order each time.

If you want to make sure everyone gets a turn at bat every inning, allow more outs per inning or make the outs meaningless, except for preventing runs. Change the rules and adapt the game to fit the needs of your group.

Centipede Race

Here is a great game that can be played indoors or outdoors. All you need are some benches and a finish line set forty to fifty feet away. Divide the group into two or more teams. Have as many young people as possible straddle the bench. When the race starts, everyone must stand up, pick up the bench (holding it between their legs), and run like a centipede. This race is a lot of fun to watch and to participate in.

Crows and Cranes

Divide the group into two teams. Designate one side as the crows; the other, the cranes. Have the two teams line up facing each other four or five feet apart. Flip a coin (heads—crows, tails—cranes) and shout the name of the team that wins the toss. If you yell "Crows!" the crows must turn around and run, with the cranes in hot pursuit. If any of the cranes succeed in touching a member (or members) of the crows before he or she crosses a given line (twenty to sixty feet away), he or she is considered a captive of the cranes and must aid the cranes when play continues. The team that captures all the members of the other team is the winner.

Bombs Away

This version of football is very simple. After the ball is hiked, everybody on the offensive team goes out for a pass—everyone is a wide receiver. No rushing the quarterback is allowed. Everyone on the defensive team is a defensive back. The quarterback can take as long to throw the pass as she or he wants. There is no running with the ball after it is caught. After a completed pass, the next play is from that point on the field. Players must rotate the quarterback position so that everyone gets to be the passer. A touchdown is scored when a pass is completed in the end zone.

David and Goliath

Divide the group into equal-size teams with the same number of boys and girls on each team and name the teams David 1 and David 2. Give each team one old nylon stocking with a whiffle ball in its toe. Invite one person of the same sex from each team to step forward to the throwing line and twirl the nylon over his or her head or at his or her side to see who can throw it the farthest. The winner gets one point for his or her team. The team with the most points wins the contest. Then repeat this contest for accuracy. As a variation, set a "Goliath" (a person, chair, or other object) approximately thirty feet from the throwing line. The person who comes the closest to hitting Goliath gets one point for his or her team. If he or she actually hits Goliath, award an additional bonus point. The players will quickly find out that it took practice for the original David to be such a skilled marksman.

Frisbasketball

The next time your group wants to play basketball, why not try this version? Instead of a basketball, use a Frisbee and as many players as you wish. Because the Frisbee cannot be dribbled, it must be advanced by passing. Basketball rules relative to penalties such as fouls, traveling, and out-of-bounds all apply. However, scoring differs: Award one point for hitting the backboard, two for hitting the square on the backboard, and three for making a goal (including foul shots). Double the scores for any shot made from beyond midcourt.

Croquet Golf

This is actually miniature golf played with a croquet set. The wickets are used instead of cups in the ground. Set up your own nine hole course by arranging the wickets around the yard. Tag each wicket with the hole number. Place small signs at each tee that tell the players where to tee off. Also indicate par for each hole. Some croquet sets include wicket tags and tee signs for playing Croquet Golf. Try to make each hole different by marking the "green" in such a way that the players can reach it only by going around shrubs, through tin cans and tires, up ramps and hills, and so on.

Frisbee Golf

Lay out a short golf course around an area designating telephone poles, light posts, fence posts, and tree trunks as holes. Set up places to tee off or designate a certain distance from the previous hole (perhaps ten feet) for the starting place. The course can be as simple or as complicated as the skill of the participants warrants. Such things as doglegs, doorways, arches, and narrow fairways add to the fun of the course. Take three or four good Frisbee throwers through the course to set the par for each hole. It is a good test of skill, but anybody can do it. Give each person a Frisbee. The object of the game is to hit all the "holes" in as few throws as possible. Direct each person to throw the Frisbee from the tee and then move to and stand where the Frisbee lands to indicate the spot for the next throw.

Whiffle Golf

Here is a crazy version of golf that young people will enjoy. Set up your own golf course on an open field, all over a campground, around houses, or just about anywhere. To make the holes, use small cans or jars just big enough for a whiffle ball. The cans can be placed on the ground and anchored there or elevated on poles. (Make nine or eighteen holes.) After the course is set, direct each player to tee off for hole number 1. No clubs are used. Players simply toss the ball underhand. If you cannot get whiffle balls, use beanbags. Each toss counts as a stroke. The idea is to get the ball into the can in the fewest possible strokes. It is best to play in foursomes, just like regular golf, to set par for each hole, to print scorecards, and so on. Consider sponsoring a Whiffle Golf tournament.

Horseyback Tag

This is a wild game that should be played on a grassy area. Each team is made up of a horse and a rider. The rider mounts the horse by jumping on the back of the horse with arms around his or her neck. The riders have a piece of masking tape placed on their back in an accessible, visible place. When a signal is given, the riders mount their horse and attempt to round up the tape on the other riders' backs. The last rider left with tape on his or her back wins. Only the riders may take the tape off other riders; the horses may not. If a horse falls, both the horse and the rider are out of the game.

Over the Line

Here is a great variation on softball. You will need a bat and a softball, six people (three on a team) and a playing field with marked boundaries (see diagram).

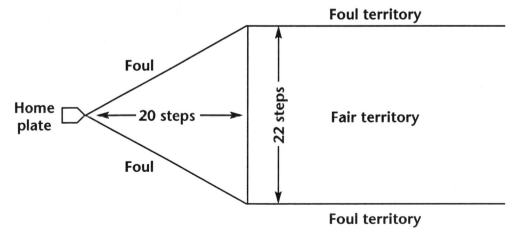

The batter stands at home plate and tries to hit the ball in the air over the line in fair territory. The pitcher is someone on the batting team. The pitcher stands anywhere she or he wants fifteen or twenty feet from the batter and lobs the ball up to be hit. The pitcher cannot interfere with the ball after it is hit. If he or she does interfere, the batter is out.

The players in the field position themselves anywhere they want in fair territory. If they catch a ball before it hits the ground, the batter is out. Anything that drops into fair territory on the fly is a base hit. A ball hit in fair territory over the heads of all three fielders is a home run.

There are no bases, so there is no base running. The bases are imaginary. When a person gets a base hit, the next batter is up. It takes three base hits (not four as in regular softball) before a run is scored. Every base hit after that adds another run. Every home run earns a bonus point. For example, a home run after the first three base hits scores four runs (clearing the bases, plus one bonus run). It takes three more base hits to start scoring runs again. Other rules follow:

- Each batter gets only two pitches to get a hit (only one foul, mis-swing, etc.). If the batter does not get a hit in two pitches, he or she is out.
- Any ball hit on the ground in front of the line is an out (unless it is foul on the first pitch).
- Each team gets three outs per inning, as in regular softball.
- The game is played for nine innings (or as many as the teams want).

Of course, the rules of the game can be modified. For example, the boundaries can be adjusted to fit the skills of the players. Or instead of using a softball, you could use a Nerf ball or a volleyball. You could play with more or fewer team members. The game is great on the beach as well as on a regular playing field. Be creative and have fun.

Shoe Kick

For this simple game, have the participants take off one shoe and hang it off the end of their foot. Have a contest to see who can kick his or her shoe the farthest. Everyone will be surprised to see how many people kick their shoes over their heads, behind them, or straight up in the air.

Tetherball Jump

For this game, have ten to twenty players form a circle. Get in the center of the circle with a tethered ball—a ball attached to a rope about eight feet long. Take the rope in your hand and begin making circles with the ball, about six inches off the ground. Have the players in the circle move in closer, and as they come within range of the whirling tether ball, they must jump over the ball. Keep the ball going faster and faster until someone fails to jump over the ball and is eliminated. Whoever remains longest is the winner. As the game progresses, you can make the ball go faster or higher off the ground. Caution: Have more than one ball twirler in case of dizziness!

Soccer Variations

Soccer is an excellent game for small youth groups because you only need teams of five or six to play. You can play following official soccer rules, or you can try one of these soccer variations.

1. Crazy soccer: This is regular soccer but with four teams and four goals. The teams can be of any size, but a minimum of two is best. The playing field should look like this:

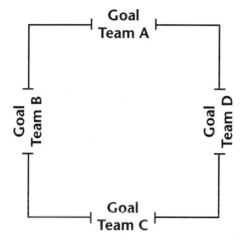

The size of the field can be determined by the number of players. Likewise, the size of the goals can vary, depending on the number of players and their skill. Goalies are optional. You can play with each team competing against the other three at the same time, or you can put two balls in play and have two games crisscrossing each other.

2. Croak ball: This variation of soccer uses an old volleyball and croquet mallets. The players must push the ball with the mallets, not swing them to hit the ball. All other soccer rules apply.

3. Monkey soccer: Play this game with a lightweight soccer ball. Regular soccer rules apply, except that the players must hit the ball underhand with their fists. This means that players will have to bend their legs and swing their arms down low, like a monkey.

4. Line soccer: Use a soft kick ball for this game. It requires two parallel lines marked on the playing field about thirty feet apart. Divide your group into two equal teams. Each team lines up behind those two lines, facing each other, leaving the center area open. Team members may not stand more than ten feet behind their lines. Players should number off on each team. One number is called, and the two players with that number go to the center. The ball is thrown into the playing area, and the two players try to kick the ball across the other team's line past all the players. The players behind the lines try to stop the ball.

Players may try to kick the ball past the team line on the other side, but only the two players whose numbers are called can be in the middle area. After a goal is scored, two new numbers are called. The people with the new number replace the first players. The game continues this way, with a new number called every minute or so.

5. Silly soccer: Instead of making goals, teams try to hit and knock pylons over with the ball to score points. The object is to knock over all the other team's pylons.

6. Solo soccer: This is the perfect soccer game for small groups in a limited area. Players stand in a circle between stakes anchored in the ground about six or eight feet apart. Pylons or chairs can also be used. The object is for each player to protect his or her own goal while trying to score through someone else's. Each person is his or her own goalie. The last person to touch the ball before it passes through a goal receives one point. The person who is scored upon receives a negative point. Goals that are kicked above the head are not counted as points.

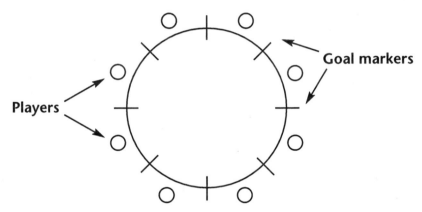

Through-the-Legs Shuffle

Here is the old "through-the-legs" game with a new twist. Have the teams line up single file behind the starting line, spreading their legs apart enough so that someone can crawl through them. Everyone must have her or his hands on the hips of the person in front of her or him. The last person crawls through the legs of the team and stands up at the front of the line. As soon as she or he stands up, the person who is now at the rear of the line crawls through. The lines move forward, and the first team to cross the goal line wins. Only one person per team can be crawling at a time.

Three Ball

This great outdoor game from New Zealand can be used with almost any age-group and any number of people. You need a baseball diamond (or a reasonable facsimile) and three balls of any kind or just about anything that can be thrown—softballs, footballs, rugby balls, soccer balls, volleyballs, Frisbees, boomerangs. The three items you use do not have to be the same. You will also need a cardboard box, a trash can, a bucket, or other container for the items.

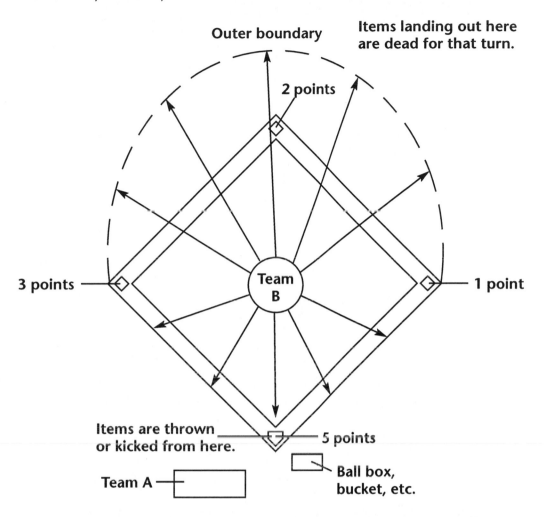

The container—"the ball box"—goes at home plate. You will need one referee to help keep score and to blow the whistle when all the balls are in. Boundaries, distance between bases, and so on, can all be adjusted depending on the size and the skill of the group.

One team is at bat, and the other team is out in the field, as in regular baseball. Everybody plays everywhere. The first batter comes to the plate and selects three balls. She or he must get rid of the three balls as quickly as possible in any way imaginable—by kicking, throwing, and so on. The balls must stay within the boundaries of the field.

After getting rid of the balls, the batter runs the bases while the team in the field tries in any way that is fast and accurate—relaying, running—to return all three balls to the box. The runner gets a point for each base and five points for a home run (making it all the way around). If a ball is caught on the fly, it is dead and does not have to be placed in the ball box. If the runner is caught between bases when the last of the three balls is placed in the box, she or he loses all accumulated points. The runner must take care to watch and stop safely on a base when all the balls are finally in.

Emphasize that there are no outs. The best way to play is to give everyone on the team a chance to play each inning and to help add up the points scored. When everybody has batted, the other team is at bat and tries to get as many points as possible. The game lasts as many innings as the players decide. With larger groups, several games can be played at once. It does not matter if the fields overlap.

Water Balloon Shot Put

This is a simple game to see who can toss a water balloon shot-put style the farthest. To give the players added incentive, the youth leader can stand as a target just out of reach of the balloons.

Water Balloon Toss

Have the players pair off. Form two lines about two feet apart, with partners standing opposite each other. Each couple gets a water balloon. At a signal, one person tosses the water balloon to his or her partner. The partner must catch it without breaking it. (An unbroken balloon may be retrieved from the ground.) If he or she is successful, each person takes one step backward. At the next signal, the balloon is again tossed. Each time one partner is successful, both move back another step. The couple whose balloon lasts the longest wins.

Tail Grab

Divide the group into any number of equal teams. Have each team form a chain, organizing a line of people in which each person grips the wrist of the one in front of him or her. The last person in the chain has a tail (a handkerchief) dangling behind. The object is for the first person in the chain to snatch the tail from another line. The fun is for each chain to maneuver to get someone else's tail while trying to keep its own.

Volleyball Variations

Volleyball is a standby for every youth group, but it can be improved and given new life by changing the rules in these ways:

1. Badminton volleyball: Get plenty of badminton rackets and play a regular volleyball game using badminton rackets and a birdie rather than a volleyball.

2. Blind volleyball: This is like regular volleyball, only the net should be a solid barrier so that neither team can see the other. Hang blankets all the way across the net. The element of surprise when the ball comes over the net makes this game fun.

3. Crazy volleyball: This is like regular volleyball, except that each team may hit the ball four times before hitting it over the net. A ball hitting the floor counts as one hit; however, the ball may not hit the floor twice in succession. These rules keep the ball in play over a long period of time.

4. Elimination volleyball: In this volleyball game, whoever makes a mistake or misses the ball goes out of the game. The teams keep getting smaller, and the team that manages to survive the longest is the winner.

5. Four-corner volleyball: This variation of volleyball involves four teams at once. You can set it up with four volleyball nets or just two, depending on the size of your teams and the number of nets available. You will need five or six poles. Arrange the nets according to one of the diagrams below. If you use two nets, form two right angles with them, as in diagram *A*. If you use four nets, tie all four to the center pole as in diagram *B*.

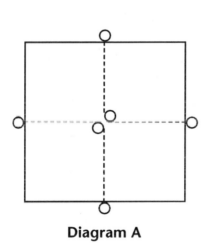

Diagram A

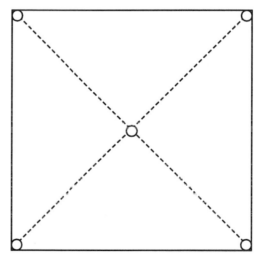

Diagram B

Position a team in each quadrant of the court. Play the game like regular volleyball, except that the players can hit the ball to all three opposing teams. Interesting strategies develop because a team is never sure exactly when the ball will be coming its way.

6. Volley volleyball: This version of volleyball uses a new way to score points. The object is for a team to hit the ball as many times as possible, up to fifty, without missing or fouling before volleying it to the opposing team. That team makes every attempt to return it without missing. If it does miss, the opposite team receives a point for each hit it made before volleying it to the team who missed. All hits must be counted audibly by the entire team or by scorers on the sidelines. Other rules for this game are as follows:

■ No person may hit the ball two consecutive times.
■ No two people may hit the ball back and forth to each other more than once in succession to increase the number of hits.

- Five points are awarded to the serving team if the opposite team fails to return a serve.
- Five points are awarded to the receiving team if a serve is missed or goes out-of-bounds or into the net.
- Players rotate on each serve, even if the serving team scores on successive serves.
- A game is fifteen minutes. The highest score wins.

7. Water volleyball: Place a pole with a sprinkler tied to the top in the middle of the volleyball net. Play a regular game of volleyball. This game would be at its best and messiest if played on a dirt surface.

8. Volley tennis: Volley Tennis is played on a tennis court with a volleyball. This variation on volleyball is a great game for any number of players and requires little athletic ability. However, it is most fun when at least a dozen people are on each team. The serve is as in regular volleyball, but the receiving team must let the ball *hit the court* before touching the ball. The receiving team is allowed three hits to get the ball back across the net, but the ball must touch the court between each hit. Only the serving team can score. Line hits are in play. The game ends at fifteen points.

9. Water balloon volleyball: For this game, use water balloons instead of a volleyball. The serving team lobs a water balloon over the net, and someone on the other side must catch it without breaking it. She or he can then toss it back over, and the serving team must catch it. All tosses must be underhanded. No spikes are allowed. If a water balloon breaks on one side of the net, the opposition scores a point. Have plenty of water balloons on hand.

10. Volley balloon waterball: This is the same as Water Balloon Volleyball, only each team gets a sheet. The entire team surrounds the sheet, holding it by the edges. On the serving team's side, a water balloon is placed in the middle of the sheet and the sheet is used to serve the balloon. The other team must catch the balloon on its sheet without breaking it and heave it back over the net to the other team. This game takes teamwork.

Sardines

This game is actually hide-and-seek in reverse. Appoint or have the group choose one person to be "It." This person hides while the rest of the group counts to one hundred (or receives a signal to begin the search). The group sets out to find the hidden person. When someone finds It, she or he hides with It instead of telling the rest of the group. The hiding place may be changed an unlimited number of times during any game. The last person to find the hidden group, which can grow to resemble a can of sardines, becomes It for the next game.

PART 5

Relays and Races

Introduction

Relays and races are perfect for small youth groups because they can be used with any number of players in any number of teams. If you have exceptionally small teams (only two or three people per team), you can make the game last longer by having each team member run the relay or race two or three times. And if your teams are unequal in size, you can make the game fair by having some players from the smaller team or teams perform twice.

All relays are basically the same: Teams line up, and each team member must run the relay course or perform specific tasks in succession. The first team to have all its members complete the relay or to complete it in the shortest amount of time is the winner.

Back Ball Relay

Teams line up. A goal (such as a chair) is placed about thirty feet in front of each team. The first two players in each line stand back-to-back. A ball, such as a basketball or a volleyball, is placed just above the belt line between them. With their arms folded in front of them, each pair must carry the ball around their goal and back to the line. Then the next two people in line go, and so on. The team that first gets all its players around the goal and back in line wins.

Three-Legged Race

Here is another favorite. Two players from each team stand side-by-side, and the left leg of one and the right leg of the other are tied together. They then race to the goal and back.

Balloon Bat Relay

Teams line up single file, and each team gets a balloon. The person at the front of each line bats the balloon with her or his hand between her or his legs, and each successive team member does the same until it reaches the last person. That person runs the balloon to the front of the line and bats the balloon down the line again. The first team to get back in its original order wins.

Back-to-Back Relay

Teams line up. The first couple in each line must stand back-to-back and be tied together with a short rope. One person runs forward, and the other runs backward to a goal. On the return trip, the person who ran forward runs backward, and vice versa. Then the next two people in line go, and so on. The team that first gets all its players around the goal and back in line wins.

Balloon Sweep Relay

Line up teams and give each team a broom and an inflated balloon. Set up a goal (such as a chair) for each team about thirty feet away. Using a broom, the first player in each line must sweep a balloon around a goal and back to the starting point. Then the next person takes the broom and balloon, and so on. The first team to get all its players around the goal and back in line wins.

Basketball Pass

Teams line up single file. The first player in each line is given a basketball. The first player passes it to the player behind him or her *over his or her head.* The next person passes it *between his or her legs* to the person behind him or her, and so on. When the last person in line gets the ball, he or she goes to the front of the line and starts the process over again. The first team to get back in its original order wins.

Basketball Squat

Divide into teams and choose captains. Have each team line up relay style about seven feet away from its captain. Each captain throws a basketball to the first person in his or her line. That person returns the throw and then squats down. Each captain then throws the ball to the second person, who does the same, and so on, down the line. To start the process from *back* to *front,* each captain throws the ball back to the last person, who must stand to catch it and remain standing after throwing it back to the captain. The basketball moves up the line until everyone has received another pass. Anytime the ball is dropped, the team must start over again. The first team to get everybody standing up again is the winner.

Ski Relay

Construct "skis" out of plywood and nail old shoes to them. Divide your group into teams and line them up relay style. The first player in each line puts on the "skis," skis to a pole, goes around it, returns to his or her team, and passes the skis on to the next person in line. The first team to get all its players around the pole and back again wins.

Broom Twist Relay

Teams line up. About twenty or thirty feet away from each team, a team leader stands holding a broom. The first player in each line runs to his or her team leader, takes the broom, and holds it against his or her chest with the bristles over his or her head. Looking up at the broom, the player must turn around as fast as possible ten times, while the leader counts the number of turns. Then the player hands the broom back to the leader, dizzily runs back to the team, and tags the next player.

Message Relay

Divide each team in half and stand the two halves in parallel lines a distance (at least ten feet, preferably more) from each other. Write a crazy message on a piece of paper for each team (sample: "Sarah Sahara tells extraordinary information to very enterprising executives"). Give a copy to the first member of each team. The person on each team who has the message reads it, wads it up, throws it on the ground, runs across the distance to the first person on his or her team in the *opposite* line, and whispers the message in his or her ear. That person then runs to the next team member in the opposite line and whispers the message to him or her, and so on, until the last person on the team hears the message. Then he or she runs to the game leader to whisper the message to him or her. The team whose final message is closest to the original message wins.

Hands Full Relay

Assemble two identical sets of at least twelve miscellaneous items (e.g., two brooms, two balls, two skillets, two rolls of bathroom tissue, two ladders). Place a set on each of two tables.

Line up a team for each table. The first player for each team runs to the team's table, picks up one item, and takes it back to the second player. Once picked up, an item cannot touch the table or the floor. The second player and each succeeding player carries the items collected by her or his teammates to the table, picks up one new item, and carries them all back to the next player. The game will begin rapidly, but the pace will slow as each player decides which item to add to a growing armload of items. It will also take increasingly longer for one player to pass her or his burden to the next player in line.

Any item that is dropped in transit or transfer must be returned to the table by the leader. No one may assist the giving and receiving players in the exchange of items, except through coaching. The first team to empty its table wins.

Caterpillar Relay

This is a good game for camp. Have the young people bring their sleeping bag and do races in them. Line up the teams relay style. The first person in each line gets in his or her sleeping bag head first and races to a certain point and back, listening to the shouted directions from his or her team. Then he or she tags the next person, and so on. The first team to finish is the winner

Coin, Book, and Ball Relay

Each team is given one quarter, one tennis ball, and a book. Each team splits up, with half its members lining up at the starting line and half at the finish line. The first person on each team balances the book on his or her head, holds the quarter in an eye, places the ball between his or her knees and walks to the finish line. No hands are to be used. He or she passes the items to a teammate at the finish line, who then performs the same task going in the opposite direction. The team continues carrying the items back and forth until each person has played.

Guzzle Relay

Teams line up single file behind a line. Each person needs a drinking straw. A gallon of apple cider is placed a certain distance away from each team. At the sound of a whistle, the first person in each line runs to the cider and starts guzzling it through the straw. When the whistle blows again, she or he stops, and the next person runs up and drinks the cider. Some people get a short drink; others, a long drink. The team that finishes its gallon of cider first is the winner.

Feather Relay

Divide the group into equal-size teams. Give each team a box of small feathers (one feather per team member). Teams line up. Across the room from each team place a small, empty box. At a signal, the first person in each line blows her or his feather the length of the room and into the box without touching the feather. Then the second players do the same, and so on. Players may blow opponents' feathers off course. The race continues until one team gets all its feathers in the box. This race can be doubly exciting if done only on hands and knees.

Forehead Race

Have the young people pair off. Each couple races to a point and back carrying a balloon between their foreheads. If the balloon is dropped, they must start over.

Gotcha Relay

Divide the group into two teams. Be sure to divide the teams so that they are about even in running ability. Set up the playing area as in the following diagram. Have each team line up single file behind its respective marker. On the signal "go," the first player of each team begins running around the track in one direction only. On completing a lap, each runner is to tag the next player on his or her team. The object of the game is to catch and tag the runner on the other team. The teams continue to run laps until a person is finally tagged. The team that catches a runner on the other team first is the winner.

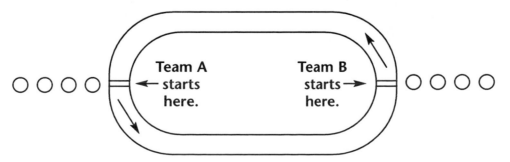

Egg Roll

Contestants roll a boiled egg along an obstacle course with their nose. If the egg cracks, a referee gives the player a new egg, and the player must start over. (Have someone peel the cracked eggs and prepare lunch!)

Frisbee Relay

This is a good outdoor relay. Divide the group into equal-size teams of five or six. Any number of teams can play at the same time. Give each team a Frisbee and have the teams spread out in a line with each team member about fifty feet or more apart. The first person throws the Frisbee to the second person, who allows the Frisbee to land, goes to where it landed, and throws it toward the third person. The object is to see which team can throw the Frisbee the greatest distance in the shortest time. Award points for throwing it the farthest and for finishing first.

Balloon Pop Relay

Teams line up single file. About twenty feet in front of each team, place a chair on which there is a balloon for each team member. One at a time, each team member runs to the chair, blows up a balloon, and sits on it to pop it. The team whose members do this in the shortest time wins.

Hand-in-Glove Relay

Teams stand in line and pass a pair of gloves from one end to the other. Use rubber kitchen gloves or large work gloves. Each person takes the gloves off the person in front of him or her and puts them on himself or herself. All the fingers of the hands must fit in the fingers of the gloves.

Lemon Relay

Teams line up in straight lines. The first person on each team is given a pencil and a lemon. He or she must push the lemon to the finish line and back using only the pencil. Then the next player goes, and so on. If the lemon goes out of a player's lane, he or she must start over.

Inner Tube Relay

Divide the group into two teams. Each team pairs off and lines up in different areas equidistant from the center of the room or the playing field. Two inner tubes are placed in the center of the playing area.

The first couple in each line runs to an inner tube, headfirst squeezes through it together, and tags the next couple, who performs the same task. The first team to have all the couples finish wins.

Lifesaver Relay

Teams line up relay style. Give each player a toothpick to hold in his or her teeth. Place a Lifesaver on the toothpick of the player at the head of each line. The team must pass the Lifesaver from toothpick to toothpick until it reaches the end of the line. If the Lifesaver is dropped before it reaches the end of the line, it must be started over again at the beginning of the line. The winning team is the one whose Lifesaver reaches the end of the line first.

Mad Relay

In this relay, each team member does something different. Teams line up single file behind a line. Opposite each team, place on a chair a bag containing slips of paper on which you have written instructions. The teams' instructions need not be identical, but make them comparable. At a signal, the first person of each team runs to the chair, draws a slip of paper, reads it, and follows the instructions on it as quickly as possible. Before returning to the team, the contestant must tag the chair. The contestant then runs back and tags the next runner. The team that uses all its instructions first is the winner. Here are a few sample instructions:

1. Run around the chair five times while continuously yelling, "The British are coming! The British are coming!"
2. Stand on one foot while holding the other in your hand, tilt your head back, and count, "10, 9, 8, 7, 6, 5, 4, 3, 2, 1, Blast off!"
3. Take your shoes off, put them on the wrong feet, and tag your nearest opponent.
4. Sit on the floor, cross your legs, and sing one verse of "Mary had a little lamb."
5. Go to an adult and make three different funny-face expressions.
6. Put your hands over your eyes and snort like a pig five times and meow like a cat five times.
7. Sit in the chair, fold your arms, and laugh loud for five seconds.
8. Run around the chair backward five times while clapping your hands.
9. Run to someone not on your team, kiss her or his hand, and gently pinch her or his cheek.

Paper Chase

Set up races in which each person is given two pieces of paper and must travel between two points stepping only on the paper.

Ping-Pong Race

Each player gets a party blower that uncoils when blown. She or he pushes a Ping-Pong ball across the floor using only the blower. The first player to blow her or his Ping-Pong ball across the finish line wins.

Potato Relay

Teams line up. Each player must push the potato along the floor to a goal and back using only his or her nose.

Sack Race

Get some old burlap bags and run some sack races. Have the young people step inside their bag, hold it up, and hop to a goal and back.

Broom Jump Relay

Team members should stand two abreast. The first couple on each team is given a broom. On "go," each one grabs one end of the broom, and they run back through their team, holding the broom just above the floor. Everyone must jump over the broom. When the couple reaches the back of the line, they must pass the broom back to the front of the line, using hands only. Then each couple repeats the relay. The first team with the original couple at the head of the line wins.

Sock Tail Relay

Make several "sock tails" and give one to each team. A sock tail consists of a belt with a sock tied onto it and a baseball in the end of the sock as a weight. By each team, put a small football on the floor. (Buy or borrow children's footballs for this relay.) The first person on each team puts on the tail with the sock hanging down behind. At a signal, the player must push the football on the floor to a goal and back with the sock tail. The next player attaches the sock, performs the task, and so on, until each team member has played. If a player touches the football with his or her feet or hands, he or she must start over.

Spoon Relay

Teams line up. Each player holds a plastic spoon in her or his mouth. The leader places a marble on the spoon of the player at the head of each line. It is passed from spoon to spoon until it reaches the end of the line. The team that gets its marble to the end of the line first is the winner.

Sucker Relay

Teams line up. Each person has a paper straw. The first person in each line picks up a piece of paper about four inches square by sucking on the straw. The paper is carried around a goal and back. Then the next person performs the task, and so on. If a player drops the paper, he or she must start over.

Thimble Relay

Teams form a line, and each player holds a straw upright in his or her mouth. The relay is started by placing a thimble on the straw of the first person in each line. The thimble is passed from player to player. The team that gets its thimble to the end of the line first is the winner.

Waddle Relay

In this relay, teams race with players carrying a small coin between their knees. Without using their hands, they must successfully drop a coin into a milk bottle or a jar placed fifteen or twenty feet away. If a player drops the coin along the way, he or she must start over.

Wagon Relay

For this game, you will need a children's wagon for each team. Also set up a slalom course for each team. Divide the group into teams and have each team pair off. Line up the teams at the start of their course and have the first couple from each team race. One person sits in the wagon and uses the handle to steer while the other person pushes him or her. When one couple finishes, the next begins. The first team to have everyone complete the course wins.

A variation is to have one person sit in the wagon while the other steers and pushes the wagon backward through the course.

Wild Wheelbarrow Race

This race requires two or more real wheelbarrows. Have your group pair off. One person pushes the wheelbarrow and the other rides in it. The pairs must travel around a goal and back. However, the wheelbarrow driver is blindfolded, and the person sitting in the wheelbarrow must give her or him directions.

Cotton Ball Relay

Each team needs a number of cotton balls in a container (such as a dish or a pan), a spatula, and an egg carton. Teams line up.

At a signal, the first person in each line picks up a cotton ball with the spatula and keeps it balanced on the spatula while running to a goal and back. If he or she loses the cotton ball, he or she must start over. When the player returns to his or her team, he or she places the cotton ball in the egg carton. Then the next player goes, and so on. The first team to fill its egg carton wins.

Weird-Barrow Race

Have your group pair off for this variation of a wheelbarrow race. Typically, in a wheelbarrow race, player 1 becomes the wheelbarrow by walking on her or his hands while player 2 uses player 1's feet as handles and runs along behind. In this race, the added difficulty is that the wheelbarrow (player 1) must push a volleyball along the ground with her or his nose.

PART 6

Special Events and Social Activities

Introduction

Each special event in this section is built around a different theme. Theme events are perhaps the most common kind of special event. For decades, people have enjoyed popular events such as the Sweethearts Banquet, the Grad Night Party, or the Sadie Hawkins Day. Holidays, too, such as Christmas, Halloween, and the Fourth of July have provided themes for socials and parties over the years.

In most cases, events of this type feature games, refreshments, decorations, costumes, and other activities centered on a chosen theme. If the event is an Old-Time Night, for example, everyone is invited to wear old-time clothes, play old-time games, hear old-time music, and eat old-time food.

Theme events can be successful with youth groups if the theme captures the imagination and sparks the interest of the young people. So pick themes that are exciting enough, crazy enough, or dumb enough to sound interesting and be fun.

For example, over the years Banana Night has become one of the most popular of all the creative theme events for youth groups. It has been done in hundreds of youth groups all across North America, and some youth groups have gone so far as to make their Banana Night an annual event. It started out as a simple idea—an evening of activities centered on the lowly banana—but as the event has evolved, it has spawned dozens of crazy games and activities, all with a banana theme.

Plan your own Banana Night, Nerd Night, or Guinness-Book-of-World-Records Night. Many young people would probably much rather come to a Noise Night than a traditional Valentine's Day party.

Although this section offers dozens of successful ideas for theme events, remember that the best theme events are those that you create yourself. Here's how.

Pick a theme—almost any theme will work. Ask the young people to think of a theme or get ideas from television (note the Fantasy Island Night in this section), the movies, popular music, or fads. Then brainstorm ideas for games, activities, events, and refreshments. You will be amazed at the results. Besides, being creative can be a lot of fun, too. The following theme events can help you begin.

Picture Party

Here is a good party idea with a photographs theme. For your publicity, send a picture of the party location, along with other details. Below are some suggested ideas for the party, but don't limit yourself to them. Any activity that incorporates the use of pictures can be used.

1. Baby picture guess: Have everyone bring a baby picture. When they arrive, collect them and post them on the wall or the bulletin board. Have the players identify each baby. You can also give awards (have the young people vote) on the cutest baby, the most unusual baby, and so on.

2. Picture scavenger hunt: Pass out magazines, divide into small scavenger-hunt teams, and give the young people a list of pictures they need to find. Pictures can include such things as a 1987 Toyota, a Swatch watch, a family on vacation, someone who looks funny (judge for the funniest), a fish, more than twenty-five people (whoever can find the most people in one picture wins), someone doing something heroic, and so on.

3. Picture identification: Ahead of time, shoot some slides or photos of various locations around town. Have the young people try to guess what they are. Some can be easy, others can be tough. Award points according to difficulty.

4. Group slide show: Show some slides of past youth group activities.

5. Group portrait: End the event by taking a group picture. Get a professional photographer to take it. Have the group pose for a serious picture as well as a crazy picture. Arrange to have enlargements made so that the participants can order them for their scrapbooks. You might want to advertise this evening in advance so that everyone is present for the group shots.

Backward Night

As the name implies, everything about this special event is done *in reverse.* Print invitations and posters backward (even from bottom to top). Invite everyone to come to this event with their clothes on backward and inside out.

Before the young people arrive, set up signs directing them to use the back door of the building. Spell everything backward.

When the participants arrive, greet them, "Good-bye, we hope you had a great time!" Continue the program exactly in reverse, so begin with prayer if you usually end with prayer. As the young people leave, put name tags on them, welcome them, and introduce visitors. If paper plates are used for refreshments, use them upside down and make everyone eat wrong-handed. Oral announcements should be made with your back to the crowd.

The games for Backward Night all require teams. Divide the group into four or more teams for all the following games. For each game, each team begins with one thousand points, and they lose points as they win.

1. Backward barnyard: Choose a different farm animal for each team. Give each person on a team the name of their barnyard animal. Turn off the lights. Have each team member mingle while making the sound of that animal in order to find the rest of his or her team. However, on Backward Night, the sounds are reversed, so the cow's sound is oooom; the dog's, wow-bow; the donkey's, haw-hee, and so on.

2. Backward charades: This game is like regular charades, but the titles must be acted out in reverse. For example, *Gone with the Wind* would be *Wind the with Gone.*

3. Backward letter scramble: Ahead of time, make four sets of cards (one set per team) with the letters *B, A, C, K, W, A, R,* and *D* on them. Pass out the cards and have each team member hold one or more cards, depending on how many members are on each team. Call out a word using those letters (e.g., *drab, raw, bark, crab*). Have the players holding those letters line up with their letters, spelling the named word *backward*. The first team to do so wins.

4. Relay games: Use any relay game you like, but run it *backward*—have the players run backward, crawl backward, or walk backward.

5. Behind-the-back pass: Teams line up shoulder-to-shoulder. Pass several objects down the line from player to player behind their back. The first team to pass a certain number of these objects to the end of the line is the winner. For fun, try using cups of water. Spilling is a penalty, and points will be added to the score.

Spy Versus Spy

This activity requires preparation and cooperation with a youth group from another church.

First, take a photo of your entire youth group (or get individual photos of each person in the group). Send the photo (or photos) to the other youth group a week or so before the event takes place. That group should send you a photo of its members, too. Show it to your group.

At a scheduled day and time, arrange for the two youth groups to go to a busy place, like a shopping mall or an airport. Initially, the two church groups should not know where the other one is. At a set time, each leader directs the groups to disperse and try to locate each other, working individually or in pairs. The young people try to find members of the other youth group by remembering them from the photo. It is up to you whether you want the young people to have access to the other group's photo, but bring it along for yourself! These rules apply: Whenever someone thinks she or he has located someone from the other group, she or he goes to that person and says, "You're under arrest!" Whoever says this key phrase first gets points for her or his group. If a person is "arrested" three times, she or he must go to "jail" (some predetermined place) and stay there for the rest of the game. The game can last thirty minutes to an hour.

If you provide names with the photo, a person can get extra points by naming the person, for example, by saying, "You're under arrest, Jennifer!" Have a party afterward with refreshments. It is a good way to get to know another youth group.

M & M's Night

This party idea makes good use of those famous little candy-covered chocolates—M & M's. (Reese's Pieces, Smarties [in Canada], or similar candies also can be used.) Give everyone a package of M & M's. Then play games like these (and make up some of your own):

1. M & M relay: Line teams up relay style. The first person on each team runs to a table where a package of M & M's is poured for him or her. He or she must eat the whole package without using his or her hands then run back and tag the next player, who runs to the table and eats M & M's, and so on.

2. M & M blowing contest: Each team must blow (yes, blow) a pile of M & M's from one point to another—ten feet away will do.

3. Find the M & M's: Divide the group into two teams. One team hides individual M & M's around the room. The other team must find as many as they can within a time limit. Make some colors worth more points than others.

4. M & M push: Have the young people push M & M's along a course with their noses, relay style.

5. M & M trading: Give each player a few M & M's, and have them trade among themselves for the colors they like best. After the trading, announce which colors are worth the most points. Or have an auction, using M & M's as money.

6. M & M gulp: Give each team of five a cup of M & M's and a paper plate. On "go," the first person on each team dumps the M & M's onto the plate and picks out and eats *only* the yellow ones. After that player places the remainder back into the cup, the second player does the same, eating only the orange ones, and so on. The team that devours its M & M's first wins. Add a penalty of five seconds for each M & M dropped on the floor.

Foot Party

Here is a great way, literally, to kick off the new year. Plan an event with a *feet* theme. Invite everyone to come to the party barefoot; absolutely no shoes are allowed. Divide into teams with names like the Toe Jams, the Bunions, and the Hangnails. Then play some of the following feet games:

1. Foot painting contest: Give teams newsprint and have them paint pictures with their feet. They can use brushes or do toe painting (finger painting with toes).

2. Foot awards: Award points and prizes for the largest foot, the smallest foot, the ugliest foot, the funniest-looking foot, and the smelliest foot.

3. Foot footage: Have teams line up with their feet toe-to-heel. The team with the longest combined length wins.

4. Foot signing: This is a ticklish mixer. Have the participants see how many autographs they can get on the bottoms of their feet.

5. Foot wrestling: Have the young people pair off and sit on the floor facing each other. Have them lock toes and try to pin the other person's foot, similar to arm wrestling.

6. Lemon pass: Teams line up, sit on the floor, and try to pass a lemon along the line and back using only their feet. The lemon cannot touch the floor.

7. Foot scramble: Divide the group into equal-size teams. Paint letters on the bottom of the players' feet, giving each team the same set of letters. When you shout a word, the players with the letters that form that word must sit down in a row with their team members and arrange their feet in order, so that the judges can read the words. To make this more challenging, print a different letter on each foot of each player.

Be imaginative and invent many other games to use the feet theme. For refreshments—how about foot-long hot dogs?

Nostalgia Night

This is a special event or party idea that can take many different forms. The idea is simply to *go back in time* for one night. You could make it an 1890s Night, a Roaring Twenties Night, a Fifties Night, or a night from any other period of time you choose. However, be certain the time period lends itself easily to getting costumes, music, decorations, and refreshments. Have everyone come dressed in period clothing, decorate the room appropriately with antiques, play music from the period (dance to it?), and show some old-time movies. Award prizes to the best-dressed person and for the most-authentic costumes. For added fun, take the whole group in their costumes to an ice-cream parlor or some other restaurant with a motif that fits your chosen time period.

Newspaper Night

Here is a good special event built around the theme of *newspapers*. To prepare for it, collect a huge pile of old newspapers, the more the better. This event could be combined with a newspaper drive. Perhaps the paper collection can take place during the day, and in the evening, you can play some of the following games. However, if you are planning to return the newspaper at the end of the evening, avoid the games that wad or use up the paper, making it unsuitable for recycling. Be aware that newsprint can soil and smear; you will need to be careful of staining clothing, carpets, and upholstery.

1. Newspaper costume race: Teams have five minutes to dress one of their players with newspapers to look like a certain character, for example, Santa Claus or Abraham Lincoln.

2. Newspaper treasure hunt: Give each team a pile of newspapers with some special slips of paper hidden in them. The first team to find them all is the winner.

3. Newspaper scavenger hunt: Call out certain items from the papers, for example, an advertisement for Chevrolet, a news item about a murder, or a baseball box score. The first team to find each wins.

4. Wad and pile contest: Teams get ten minutes to wad up all their paper into a big pile. The team with the highest pile wins.

5. Hide and seek: Hide as many players as possible under the pile of wadded-up newspapers. The team with the most people under the paper and out of sight is the winner.

6. Compact newspapers: Teams try to compact their pile of paper into as small a pile as possible.

7. Snowball fight: Divide the group into two teams. Make a line of chairs between them. Teams are given time to wad up all their paper into snowballs. At a signal, they throw as many snowballs as possible over to the other team's side. When the whistle blows, everyone stops. The team with the least amount of paper on its side is the winner.

8. Disposal event: Give every team plastic trash bags. Make a contest out of putting all the newspaper into the bags. The team that fills the most bags is the winner.

Strobe Mania Night

Get a strobe light and play these three games with it. Most strobes have an adjustment for higher and lower sequencing (greater or lesser intervals between flashes), which makes the following activities fun—especially if you videotape them and replay them for the group.

1. Creature feature: Set the strobe at a high rate and position it about forty feet from where the kids do their thing. For the trick to work, of course, you need total darkness. Have the young people shuffle their feet across the room as rapidly as they can, one at a time. Ask the rest of the group to simply watch as the strobe is turned on. The result is the illusion of a person floating across the room. See who can do it the best. Creativity and video replay make this one a lot of fun.

2. Surprise tag: Set the strobe at a low rate. Have participants play tag. They will appear to mysteriously move from one spot to another and will be harder to tag.

3. Trampoline delight: Use a small exercise trampoline and cover it with a piece of dark cloth. Then have the young people do the Creature Feature (see above) and end by bouncing up on the trampoline. They will appear to suddenly shoot into the air.

Banana Night

To advertise Banana Night, put up signs and posters inviting participants to go bananas on Banana Night. Have the young people wear banana colors—yellow, green, or brown (overripe). Announce that their ticket to the event can be one banana, which will be cut in half like a normal ticket at the door. As the young people arrive, give them banana stickers of the major brands of bananas (these are available from your local produce distributor) to place on their body. Decorate the room in "Early American Banana."

After the participants arrive, divide them into bunches and play any of the following games. Remind the young people that bananas are food and should be treated as such and not wasted.

1. Banana relay: Divide the group into four teams. Line them up in a square, sitting on chairs or on the floor. Each team makes up one side of the square. A chair or some other marker is placed in the middle of the square. An edible banana is given to each team. At a signal, the first person on each team takes the banana, runs around the center chair, and takes the vacant seat at the opposite end of her or his team line. Meanwhile, the rest of the team scoots down one seat. Then the banana is passed down the line from person to person until it reaches the new first person in line, and the game continues. The first team to get everyone back in their original chair *and* to have their first runner eat the banana wins.

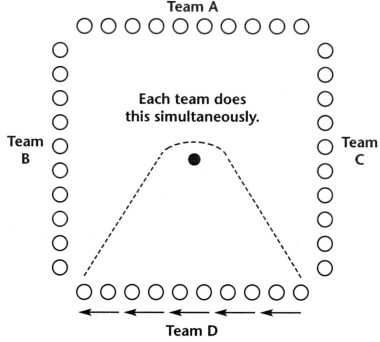

2. Bobbing for bananas: Bananas float, so you can bob for them.

3. Shoot-out at the O.K. Banana: Have contestants stick a banana in their holster (pocket) and quickdraw it as if they were in a gunfight. When they draw their banana, they peel it and eat it. The first shooter with an empty mouth is the winner.

4. Pass the banana: Each team sits in a circle with the players' feet toward the center. At a signal, a banana is passed from one person to another via feet. If the banana is dropped, the person who dropped it becomes the beginning of a new circle, and the banana must be passed completely around again. Each team is timed, starting over if the banana is dropped. The team with the shortest time wins.

5. Doctor the banana: Each team is given a banana, a knife, and several toothpicks. Within an agreed time limit, each team performs open banana surgery by carefully peeling the banana and slicing it into four equal pieces for a judge to verify the cuttings. Then the patient is cured by using the toothpicks to put the banana back together again. The team with the most "cured" banana wins.

6. Banana eating contest: Each team selects a person to represent them. Place a peeled banana with one end in the person's mouth. The first person to eat the banana without using hands wins.

7. Couples' banana eat: Couples face each other with a banana placed on a table between them. At a signal, they must peel and eat the banana without using their hands. They must do everything with their teeth. It's a riot to watch.

8. Banana fashion show: All you need are a few bananas and some paper doll clothes (or pictures of clothes from magazines and catalogs). Each person dresses her or his banana to enter the fashion show.

9. "All My Bananas": Using their fashion show bananas, the young people write three-minute soap operas. Then teams compete for the most gripping dramatic presentation.

10. Custom banana hot rod show: Give each team a model-car kit to customize their banana to enter the Custom Banana Hot Rod Show. If two or more teams design their banana with wheels, they can enter the Banana Hot Rod Grand Prix. Let each team roll their car down an incline. The champ is the banana that reaches the bottom first or goes the farthest.

11. Banana videos: Using video cameras, each group makes a real video with their banana puppets. The bananas can lip-sync popular songs.

12. Banana air band contest: The young people lip-sync records using bananas as instruments. This contest should be videotaped.

13. Banana feet relay: Participants line up relay style and sit down facing one direction. The first person picks up the banana with his or her feet, rolls over straight-backed, then "hands off" the banana to the next person, who takes it from that person's feet using only his or her feet. The last person peels the banana and eats it. If this is done in teams, the first to finish is the winner.

14. Capture-the-banana: Play Capture-the-Flag, only use bananas.

For refreshments, what else? Banana splits!

Garbage In, Garbage Out Party

The theme of this game is *trash, garbage, junk,* and *rubbish.* Ask the young people to come dressed in their worst clothes and try these games:

1. Trash scavenger hunt: Divide the group into teams. Send each team out with a large bag and a list of stuff that has been, is going to be, or should have been discarded or put into a recycling bin. The team that returns with the most items within a specified period of time wins.

2. A bigger and worser hunt: Teams start with some item of trash and run around the neighborhood trying to trade down for something worse at each house. The team that returns with the worst trash is the winner.

3. Garbage-bag volleyball: Actually, many games can be played with these big plastic bags. But for this game, fill one up with air, tie it off, and use it as a volleyball.

For refreshments, ask parents to provide plenty of leftovers. Be creative, and you can make this the absolute worst event of the year!

Progressive Dinners

Normally a progressive dinner is done by transporting the group from one place to another with a different course (appetizer, soup, salad, main course, dessert) served at each location. But you might want to try one of these creative variations:

1. Backward progressive dinner: The meal is served in reverse order, and everything else is done backward, too. People should wear their clothes inside out, walk backward, and so on. Use your imagination.

2. Bike progressive dinner: Progress from house to house on bikes. Or try something else, like roller skating or walking backward.

3. International progressive dinner: For each course, prepare food from a different country (e.g., Mexico, China, Germany, Italy, and France).

4. Dessert progressive dinner: Feature a different dessert at each location.

5. Fast-food progressive dinner: Travel from one fast-food restaurant to another; begin with an appetizer (french fries) and progress to salad, drink, main course, and dessert.

6. Treasure hunt progressive dinner: Participants must solve clues to discover the location of the next course of the meal. This adds a little excitement and competition to the event.

Tater Night

Here is a fun special event centered around the theme of *potatoes*. Advertise it with slogans such as Don't be a Vegi-Tater or a Hesi-Tater . . . Come to Tater Night! Get some potato sacks and make shirts out of them. Have everyone bring a few potatoes as their admission. Give an award to whoever brings the biggest potato, the ugliest potato, and the most beautiful potato. Then play some of these potato games:

1. Tater contest: Have a Tater-tasting contest, using several different brands of potato chips (you can usually find at least a dozen different brands in local supermarkets). To make a contest, place the chips in numbered bowls and see if the contestants can match the chips with the brand names. As a variation, use french fries from various fast-food restaurants.

2. "The People's Tater": This skit is a takeoff on the TV show "The People's Court." You will need twelve different people to play the Tater Family (members of the jury) listed below and one person to be Judge Tater. Each Tater family member must respond to questions in such a way as to reveal his or her personality. As the jury is asked questions by Judge Tater, the rest of the group tries to guess what personality each Tater is exhibiting. Afterward, reveal the tater names:

Spec-Tater	Irri-Tater
Hesi-Tater	Facili-Tater
Devas-Tater	Agi-Tater
Commen-Tater	Cogi-Tater
Dic-Tater	Vegi-Tater
Imi-Tater	Medi-Tater

3. Mr. Potato Head race: Divide the group into teams—the number of teams will depend on the number of Mr. Potato Head games you have available (check your local toy store). The object of the game is for each team to put together their Mr. Potato Head successfully. Teams line up single file about twenty feet from Mr. Potato Head. The first person on each team is blindfolded. She or he runs to Mr. Potato Head and adds a part. Then the next person is blindfolded, and so on. The first team to finish or whichever team has the best-looking Mr. Potato Head at the end of the time limit is the winner.

4. Baked potatoes scramble: Write the words *baked potatoes* on a chalkboard or a large piece of butcher paper. Have the young people pair off and see which pair can come up with the most words using only the letters in these words. Each letter can be used only as many times as it appears in these two words.

5. Potato push: Have the young people push a potato along the ground in a figure-eight course, using only their heads (noses, chins, foreheads). Give everyone a potato and have them all push together. It's really fun to watch.

All sorts of ball games and relays can also be played with potatoes, like potato football. Divide the group into teams using potato names, such as the Russets, the Idahos, the Scallops, and the Hash Browns. Serve gourmet baked potatoes for a delicious way to end (or begin) the evening.

Scavenger Hunts

A scavenger hunt is always fun for a small youth group. The concept is simple: You give the participants a list of items, and they go out and bring back as many items on the list as possible within the time limit. They can hunt in groups of two or three, or they can hunt in larger teams. After the hunt is over, you can have a party, award prizes to the winners, play some other games, and serve refreshments.

You can make any scavenger hunt new by changing its theme or doing it in a new way. Here are a few great scavenger hunt ideas:

1. Polaroid scavenger hunt: Divide your group into two teams and give each team an instant camera, a couple rolls of film, and a list of pictures that they have to take, develop, and bring back. Pictures can be worth more or less points, depending on the difficulty of locating the subject. The list can include things like "your group up in a tree," "your group in the backseat of a police car," or "your group riding the escalator in the shopping mall."

2. Sound scavenger hunt: This is like the Polaroid Scavenger Hunt, except that you give each team a cassette tape recorder, a blank tape, and a list of sounds that they must record and bring back. Sounds can include "a dog barking," "a police siren," "a cuckoo clock," or "someone over sixty-five who can explain what the term 'heavy metal' means."

3. Scriptural scavenger hunt: Participants must bring back items that can be found in the Bible and produce a Bible verse that specifically mentions it.

4. Crazy creative scavenger hunt: Give each scavenger team a list of items that do not make sense, such as a "dip flipper," a "giant wahoo," a "yellow grot grabber," a "snail egg," or a "portable electric thumb twiddly dummer." Encourage the participants to bring back items that they think fit the descriptive names. A team of judges can determine which team actually brought back the "real" item.

5. Action scavenger hunt: Give each team a list of things they must *do*, like "Sing a verse of 'Amazing Grace,'" "Run around the house twice," "Get a guided tour of the kitchen," or "Sweep the garage." Have them go to various homes and perform these tasks and ask the people at each house to sign their sheet to verify that they actually accomplished the action. Make a rule that only one action per house is allowed.

6. The great race: Give each team a list of questions that they must answer at various locations, such as "Who made the light pole on the corner of Main and Broadway?"; "How many light bulbs are burnt out on the Pizza Parlor sign at Fifth and Mapleview?"; "How many red lights are flashing on the KSON radio tower?" They must return with as many correct answers as possible.

7. Pizza scavenger hunt: Have the participants try to collect pizza ingredients on their scavenger hunt. When they return, have a pizza party.

8. People scavenger hunt: Give each group a list of people to either bring back with them or just autograph their sheet. For example: "someone over six feet tall," "someone with braces on their teeth," "someone who can play a banjo," "someone on the football team," or "someone who has a twin brother or sister."

Retreats and Easy Overnighters

All kinds of overnight events are easy to do with a small youth group. Here are a few examples:

1. Lock-in: This is essentially a slumber party held at the church. Have the young people bring their sleeping bags to camp out inside the church building. Play games, show movies, have plenty of snacks. They will love it.

2. Tent retreat: Find a local campground and borrow or rent enough tents for your group. It is a great way to do a weekend retreat without the normal expense of securing a retreat center.

3. Backpacking: Most national forests allow a maximum of twelve to fifteen people per group into the backcountry areas, so backpacking makes an excellent overnight trip for a small youth group. In most cities, you can find places from which to rent all the gear you need. It is a great experience for the participants.

4. Motel retreats: A small youth group can have an outstanding retreat using a small motel that has a swimming pool, a meeting room, and a restaurant. Many small motels offer rooms at reasonable rates.

Recreational Activities

Here are some ideas for special events that involve games and recreation:

1. Skating party: Go to a local skating rink or have all the young people bring their skates to the church and use the church parking lot for a variety of games on skates.

2. Miniature golf: Most cities and towns have one or more miniature golf courses that offer challenging and interesting golf games. Some also offer batting cages, video games, and other activities.

3. Tournament: Your youth group can sponsor a volleyball tournament, a racquetball tournament, a tennis tournament, or a bowling tournament. Invite other groups.

4. Square dance: A square dance is a lot of fun for youth groups. Many young people may think of it as hokey, but if you can get a good caller and promote it with enthusiasm, they will be surprised at how much fun it can be. Invite other groups.

5. Game day: Have a day or an evening of games like those provided in this book. Call it "Super Saturday" or a "R.I.O.T." (Ridiculous, Incredible, Outstanding, and Terrific!)

6. Bike events: Have a bike hike or a bike rodeo.

7. Ski trips: Go snow skiing or waterskiing.

8. Jog-a-thon: Many young people enjoy running for fitness and fun, so set up opportunities to jog together.

Apathy Party

The theme of this event is (ho hum) *boredom*. Carried to its extreme, it can be a million laughs and anything but boring. Advertise it in the most *boring* ways possible, which actually will attract a lot of attention. Ask the young people to dress as if they just did not care—to wear the blandest and most-boring clothes they can imagine.

When the young people arrive, have the leaders greet them at the door and hand out a list of rules for the party (see "Apathy Party Rules"). Give the leaders a few paper bags large enough to put over the heads of anyone who laughs, gets excited, or shows any enthusiasm whatsoever.

The following games can be played at this party:

1. Undramatic reading: Have a phone book or a dictionary available. Ask each person to read a selection from the material as unemotionally and dully as possible. Judges determine the winner.

2. Clothes judging: Have everyone line up and ask the youth leaders to judge everyone's clothing. The winner will be the person with the blandest outfit. (Do this only if the participants have been forewarned to dress dully.)

3. Deadpan-face-staring: Have everyone pair off, and at the signal, ask the participants to try to outstare their partner. Announce that the winner is the one who stares the longest without laughing, looking away, or closing her or his eyes. Note that blinking is permitted. Urge the contestants to say things to get their partner to laugh.

4. Balancing-air-on-a-spoon relay: Announce a relay in which the players are to balance air on a spoon. Play the relay normally, but have the leaders determine who has dropped the air off her or his spoon and ask her or him to start over again. The first team to finish is disqualified for trying too hard. The last-place team is disqualified for trying to lose.

Other games can be played in a similar fashion, or you can announce that the rest of the games were canceled due to lack of interest. Conclude with some boring slides, boring movies, or boring skits. Present awards for the most-boring activities in your youth group. Serve some lukewarm, half-baked refreshments—for example, flat soda pop and melted ice cream. It may taste bland, but your group will love it.

Apathy Party Rules

Not Allowed

- laughing (giggling, chuckling)
- crying
- smiling (grinning)
- frowning (scowling)
- loud voices (neither happy nor angry)
- fast movements
- bright eyes
- enthusiastic hand gestures
- applause
- interesting conversations
- exclamations (wow, oh boy)

Allowed

- yawning
- bored looks (glazed eyes, rolling eyes)
- slow movements
- tapping fingers
- twiddling thumbs
- monotone voice
- boring conversations
- staring into space
- sleep

Note: If you are caught breaking the rules, you must put a paper bag over your head until you are able to control yourself and behave in a properly bored manner. An adult will decide this. Have a real ho-hum time.

Hallelujah Hoedown

Depending on where you live, your young people may enjoy an event centered around the theme of *hillbillies*. It is especially effective if combined with a real, old-fashioned hayride. Activities could include the following:

1. Hillbilly fashion show: Have the young people come dressed as hillbillies and award prizes to the best-dressed hillbillies.

2. The corn-fusion game: This is like the old game of Confusion, where you give players a list of about eight things they have to do in any order they wish. Create your own game but give it a hillbilly theme. Here are some sample tasks:

■ Find someone who has used a real outhouse. He or she initials here: _____

■ Get three people together and call hogs for ten seconds as loudly as you can. One of them initials here: _____

■ Find someone to be a plow. You hold her or his legs while she or he walks on her or his hands. Plow a furrow about ten feet long. She or he initials here: _____

3. The barnyard game: Choose a different farm animal for each team. Secretly assign each person on a team the name of their barnyard animal. Turn off the lights. Everyone mingles around the room making the sound of her or his animal. All those making the same sound must get together and lock arms. The first group to find all its members is the winner. For fun, have only one person be the donkey.

4. Hillbilly talent competition: Have the young people come prepared to compete for prizes. Talent must be authentic hillbilly talent, such as banjo picking, yodeling, cow-chip tossing, hog calling, nose singing, knee slapping, and putting together a bottle band.

Plan a barbecue and serve good country vittles—mashed potatoes and biscuits, black-eyed peas, and corn-on-the-cob. Have a few freezers of homemade ice cream ready to crank. Decorate with a country motif and provide some country or bluegrass music for atmosphere. Sometimes an event like this is actually most popular with young people who live in the city because it is a good change of pace.

PART 7

Service Projects for Small Youth Groups

Introduction

Inevitably, small youth groups feel lifeless sometimes simply because the group is so small. One of the best ways to revitalize a struggling youth group is to challenge the young people to be involved in ministry and service to others.

No youth group is too small to do great things for God. All God needs is the availability of your young people and their willingness to be used. Mission and service are good ways to enliven a small youth group.

Adopt a Grandparent

This service project is for young people who are mature enough to make a long-term commitment. The first step is to take the entire group to visit a nursing home. Allow the young people to mingle and talk with these people so that they get to know them better.

Afterward, introduce them to the idea of adopting one or more of these seniors as grandparents. Assign each young person (or have them choose) one or two elderly people to visit on a regular basis, to remember on special occasions, to take on short trips—in a word, to befriend. This friendship commitment can continue for a specific amount of time, perhaps a year or maybe even longer.

During the course of the project, the young people can share with one another how things are going and what problems they are encountering. The adult youth leaders need to monitor the project and offer help and encouragement to the young people. At the end of the project or at the end of the year, the group can sponsor a special banquet. Most young people will find this project rewarding, and the older people will too.

Rake and Run

This is a service project that young people and the neighborhood enjoy. Ahead of time, consult your parish's social-action people and procure a list of people (older people, needy people) who would appreciate and welcome having their lawn raked. On a given day, gather all the members of the youth group to rake leaves. Ask them to bring their own rakes. Load everybody into the church bus and cruise up and down streets looking for houses that want and need to have their leaves raked. With fifteen or twenty people, it will only take five minutes to rake and bag the leaves.

Remind the participants that they are on other people's property and that they should be careful of the shrubbery and other property. When the job is finished at each house, have the young people leave a calling card that offers best wishes and lets the people know who they are. Most people are impressed and grateful, and the young people feel good about what they have done.

During the winter, this event can be called "Snow and Blow" (shoveling snow off people's sidewalks). During the spring, call it "Splash and Split" (washing people's windows), in the summer, "Mow and Blow" (mowing people's lawns). In each case, the idea is to give an unexpected act of kindness to others.

Letter-Writing Campaigns

Never underestimate the importance of organizing a letter-writing campaign on an important social or political issue. Congresspeople and candidates are very much influenced by the flow of mail. The letters should all address themselves to the issue, and they should state whether they are for or against a particular piece of legislation. But each person should write the letter in her or his own words and style.

Bread for the World is one organization that attempts to keep Christian people aware of important legislation affecting poor and needy people of the world. This organization encourages churches to send an "offering of letters" to local members of congress to influence them about the production and distribution of food. Even though in some cases the volume of mail may be too great to read, a careful record is always kept of letters for or against every issue. Representatives and senators vote on the basis of that record.

Ministry to Persons with Mental Retardation

Most cities have institutions that care for disabled persons or persons with mental retardation. In many cases, these institutions are under-staffed and operate on a shoestring budget. They can provide a wide variety of opportunities for ministry.

Preparation is always important when doing service projects, but especially so with ministry to people with mental retardation. Young people who are totally unprepared may become frightened or upset at the actions or conditions of people with mental retardation. Begin by simply visiting a home for people with mental retardation. A staff person can help your group with their questions and concerns.

Here are a few activities that will establish and nurture bonds between your young people and persons with mental retardation:

1. Bring music. People with mental retardation often listen to music with an intensity that is surprising. Guitars or other instruments will be a hit.

2. Play games. Frisbee throwing, ball games, active games of all kinds are great.

3. Have your young people bring some arts and crafts projects that they can work on with the residents.

4. Have individuals develop a relationship with one person. Have them help him or her with letter writing and other tasks that may be difficult. Suggest that your young people go for walks with that person and take him or her to new places or engage in recreational activities. In most cases, people with mental retardation are allowed to leave their residence if they have supervision.

5. Celebrate the Eucharist or prayer services at the institution.

6. Involve your young people in a Special Olympics. This nationally known event is conducted in local communities all over the country. Most institutions need volunteers who will be coaches, helpers, and escorts.

7. Bring a few young people who are mentally retarded to your youth group meetings. You will find that they will contribute a great deal to your group.

Puppet Ministry

Puppet ministry is popular with youth groups. Develop a good puppet program, complete with a wide selection of Muppet-style hand puppets, scenery, and props. Several companies produce puppets, scripts, recorded programs, and sound equipment. Seminars are also available that instruct people how to put on professional puppet shows.

Once your group has both puppets and a program, take it out to underprivileged areas where there are a lot of children—the inner city, an American Indian reservation, or a children's hospital. Produce a fun, entertaining program, and you will find that many of your young people will get excited about this kind of ministry.

Convalescent Home Ministry

Hundreds of thousands of older people reside in convalescent hospitals (nursing homes) all over the country. In most cases, they are there because they need regular medical or nursing care. These residences provide youth groups with a tremendous opportunity for service. It is likely that several convalescent homes located close to your church or community would love to have your group involved in voluntary service.

Most convalescent homes have an activities director who will gladly give you information and help you plan whatever you choose to do. Begin by contacting this person or the administrator of the convalescent home to find out whether the services of your group would be welcomed. Most convalescent homes have a difficult time finding people to come and do things for their patients, and often the patients especially enjoy young people. The activities director will probably be available to present an orientation program for the youth group.

Even though some of the people in convalescent homes are losing many of their physical abilities, they are basically just like everyone else. They enjoy being around people; they respond to a smile, a touch, kind words, music, and laughter. Your youth group can provide these things for men and women who often feel isolated from the outside world. The following list of possible activities is directed to the young people themselves. Make copies and give them to the young people *or* set up your program so that the young people take the initiative.

There is really no limit to the things that young people can do in a convalescent home. Think creatively and take advantage of this crucial ministry that is close to home. If you are not aware of any convalescent homes in your area, check the yellow pages of your telephone directory, meet with your local doctor, or contact the American Health Care Association (1200 Fifteenth Street NW, Washington, DC 20005) for a listing of local and state nursing home associations.

Convalescent Home Ministry

1. Begin one-on-one visits with someone living in a convalescent home, perhaps as part of an "Adopt a Grandparent" program. These visits can include conversing, reading aloud, writing letters, or just being a good listener.

2. Take the residents on short trips. Most residents of convalescent homes are permitted to leave the hospital for field trips, such as going to a restaurant, a movie, a high school football game, or church. Some convalescent homes plan their own outings for their people, and your group can help. Sometimes all that is needed is someone to push the residents around the block or even around the parking lot.

3. Call the older people on the phone. Most residents of convalescent homes enjoy talking to someone who is interested in them. Once your young people have established a relationship in person, a regular phone-calling program can work both ways—with the young people calling the residents, and the residents knowing that they are free to call their young friends anytime.

4. Stage musical performances, plays, and skits at the convalescent home. Use the meeting hall at a local nursing home for your regular youth group meeting and invite the patients to participate. Provide or participate in liturgy or paraliturgy for the convalescent home.

5. Provide music for the residents. If you have any young people who are talented in music, encourage them to share their music (especially the familiar old hymns and songs the older people grew up with).

6. Play games with convalescent home residents. Most of the patients like playing games such as Scrabble, checkers, or dominoes.

7. Provide gifts for the older people. Like most people, they enjoy receiving gifts now and then. For example, a baseball cap to protect their head when they go outside, a pouch that they can hang on the side of their wheelchair to keep things in, a small bouquet of flowers, a book, or a tape. They also enjoy giving gifts, and they will.

8. Bring pets or small children to the convalescent home. Because of the nature of the home, most of the residents are not given the opportunity to hold a small animal or to touch a small child. Something as ordinary as that can be a great source of joy for an older person who is confined to a nursing home.

9. Plant a garden for the patients. Usually, a small plot will be available at or near the convalescent home where you can prepare the soil and plant a garden. Invite the residents to choose what they would like to plant. Expect them to help take care of the garden, too. Most people look forward to watering their plants and watching them grow; older people are no exception to this rule.

Sponsor a Child

Many agencies, such as World Vision and Compassion International, try to find financial sponsors for children in orphanages overseas. Usually these agencies ask for money to provide food, clothing, and shelter for children. Most of the time you can select a child to sponsor by name and receive detailed information about the child, including photos and sometimes handwritten thank-you notes from the child.

Why not ask your church group to adopt one of these children and pledge to support the child on a monthly basis? Each person in the youth group can give a certain amount per month and pray for this child on a regular basis. Since the child's progress can be monitored by the entire group, the young people will feel involved in that child's life. This kind of project helps young people develop a world awareness and a sense of compassion for others.

Trash Bash

Collecting trash from streets and vacant lots is a valuable community service project. Divide your group into teams of five or six each and assign them different areas of the community. Have each person carry a heavy-duty trash bag and wear gloves. Designate a couple of the bags on each team for recyclables. Have the young people tie the bags of garbage and place them in large dumpsters provided by a trash collection company. Have them sort the recyclables and take them to a recycling center.

One group turned this into a marathon event, with participants taking turns working around the clock to establish a record of two hundred consecutive hours of trash collecting. Usually something like this attracts the attention of local news media and city officials, who give the group encouragement and praise.

Service Scavenger Hunt

This scavenger hunt moves the emphasis from getting to giving. Give each team a list of items: "Mow someone's lawn," "Clean all the windows on the front of someone's house," "Empty all the wastebaskets in someone's home," or "Wash someone's car." Make sure the young people get permission and do a good job at each location.

Letters to the Editor

On crucial political issues, have your group write letters to the editor of the local newspaper. These are usually published and read by hundreds, sometimes thousands, of people, including candidates and policymakers. Letters provide a significant forum for expressing political views from a Christian perspective. Advise your young people to sign their letters and not to sign them in such a way that it looks like it comes from the entire group or church. That would not be honest or fair to those who may not share the young people's views.